FRAMING THE FUTURE

Working Effectively with Intelligent Technology — With Soul

by

Joseph J. Bonocore

Author: Joseph J. Bonocore

author@bonocore.com

415-845-8692

Book3.v4

9/5/2025

Table of Contents

Dedication

To Phyllis, my wife --- whose steadiness, brilliance, and grace make every threshold lighter to cross. You are the quiet wisdom behind every word I write.

To my children --- Joseph, Kristen, and Michael --- whose lives remind me that innovation begins not in systems, but in questions... the kind only a curious heart can ask.

To my brother, Robert Bonocore and his wife, Judith Bonocore whose actions remind me of the true meaning of family and their life long support of all my efforts

For all of you: this book carries the rhythms of our home, the cadence of our conversations, and the soul of our shared journey.

Acknowledgments

This book is the result of many quiet collaborations, seen and unseen.

To Phyllis --- my life's anchor and compass. Your presence steadies my rhythm, your wisdom shapes my thought, and your love is woven into every page. I am endlessly grateful.

To Joseph, Kristen, and Michael --- you remind me daily that curiosity is a sacred force. Your questions have sharpened mine, and your stories continue to reshape how I see the world.

To my extended family --- especially those whose voices shaped my early cadence, table conversations, and sense of belonging. Your legacy lives inside every story told here.

To mentors and colleagues across decades of teaching, consulting, and design --- thank you for your questions, your insight, and your trust. You challenged me to go deeper and lead soulfully.

To the teams, students, and professionals who engaged this material in its earliest form --- your reflections turned theory into rhythm. You helped shape this manuscript's heartbeat.

And finally, to every reader who arrives with openness, story, and hope --- I see you. I wrote this for you.

Foreword

"We stand at a threshold where the question isn't whether machines can think, but whether we can relate to them in ways that preserve what makes us human."

You hold in your hands more than a book about artificial intelligence or professional development. This is an invitation to reimagine our relationship with technology itself—to move beyond the familiar debates about efficiency versus humanity and discover what becomes possible when we approach intelligent systems as collaborators rather than competitors, as mirrors for our values rather than replacements for our judgment.

Joseph Bonocore writes from a place of deep cultural grounding. His Italian-American heritage infuses every page with the understanding that the most important work happens around tables where people truly see each other, where stories carry moral weight across generations, and where wisdom emerges through relationship rather than algorithm. This cultural lens transforms what could have been another technology guide into something far more essential: a meditation on how we preserve soul in an age of artificial intelligence.

In these pages, you'll discover that the future of human-AI collaboration won't be determined by who masters the latest tools or writes the cleverest prompts. Instead, it will belong to those who understand that technology without cultural wisdom becomes hollow optimization, that efficiency without emotional intelligence creates burnout rather than breakthrough, and that innovation without ethical foundation serves no purpose worthy of human attention.

Bonocore demonstrates something revolutionary: that artificial intelligence reveals its greatest potential not when it replaces human thinking, but when it enhances human wisdom. Through frameworks tested in real organizations and relationships built over decades of consulting and teaching, he shows how emotional architecture shapes every meaningful interaction, how storytelling transforms information into insight, and how authentic visibility differs profoundly from digital surveillance.

This book emerges from lived experience rather than theoretical speculation. Each chapter reflects years of helping organizations navigate the complex terrain where human judgment meets artificial capability, where cultural inheritance intersects with technological innovation, and where ancient wisdom about relationship and community provides guidance for unprecedented challenges.

Whether you're a leader wondering how to maintain humanity in increasingly automated environments, a professional seeking to work authentically with AI tools, or simply someone who senses that our technological future requires more than faster processing and better algorithms, these insights will resonate deeply. Bonocore offers neither technophobic resistance nor uncritical embrace, but rather a third path: conscious partnership that honors both human dignity and artificial capability.

The chapters ahead will challenge you to think differently about visibility and vulnerability, about innovation and inheritance, about what it means to lead with both intelligence and soul in environments where machines increasingly participate in decisions that shape human lives and communities.

More than guidance for working with AI, this book provides a framework for being fully human in technological spaces—for preserving the cultural wisdom, emotional intelligence, and moral imagination that no algorithm can replicate, while leveraging artificial capability to serve purposes larger than individual productivity or organizational efficiency.

The future isn't something that happens to us. It's something we frame through countless daily choices about how to relate to each other and to the intelligent systems that increasingly mediate our work, our creativity, and our connections. This book invites you to frame that future with intention, with cultural grounding, and with the understanding that soul isn't something technology threatens—it's something technology desperately needs.

Welcome to a conversation about making that future worthy of the wisdom we've inherited and the communities we're here to serve.

—*Editors*

PART I

Foundations Of Soulful Technology

CHAPTER 1

Introduction: A New Partnership Begins

I. Awakening to a New Kind of Colleague

"What if your most insightful colleague never sleeps, learns faster than anyone you know, and has no heartbeat—but still mirrors your humanity?"

The rhythm of modern work has changed. Today, we wake not only to devices, but to digital companions who listen, interpret, and collaborate. These systems anticipate tone. They speak our language. They remember our preferences. No longer passive tools waiting for commands, these technologies are becoming interactive minds—reframing how we create, learn, and lead.

This transformation didn't arrive with fanfare. Instead, it emerged through subtle shifts: the moment when autocorrect began suggesting not just spelling, but sentiment. When search engines started finishing our thoughts. When recommendation systems began to know us better than we knew ourselves.

We are no longer simply automating tasks. We are forming relationships—with algorithms trained on data, nuance, ethics, and voice. These digital companions understand context. They adapt to our rhythms. They offer insights that surprise us with their relevance.

But this partnership requires more than technical proficiency. It demands emotional intelligence, ethical clarity, and the wisdom to know when to lead, when to follow, and when to pause. The question isn't whether these intelligent systems can think—it's whether we can relate to them in ways that preserve and amplify our humanity.

II. The Arc of Technology: From Mechanism to Presence

To understand this shift, we must trace technology's evolutionary arc.

The Industrial Age taught us to amplify muscle through machinery. Steam engines moved mountains. Assembly lines multiplied output. The partnership was physical—we provided direction, machines provided power. Success was measured in tons moved, products manufactured, distances covered.

The Information Age extended our cognition through computing. Databases became external memories. Spreadsheets automated calculations. The internet connected minds across continents. The partnership became intellectual—we provided questions, computers provided answers. Success was measured in information processed, connections made, knowledge shared.

Now we enter **the Intelligence Age**, where technology reflects insight through collaboration. These systems don't just store or calculate—they interpret, suggest, and co-create. They understand context, recognize patterns we miss, and offer perspectives that challenge our assumptions. The partnership becomes intuitive—we provide purpose, intelligence provides possibility.

This evolution represents more than technological advancement. It reflects a fundamental shift in how we understand consciousness, creativity, and collaboration. We're moving from a world where we use tools to a world where we partner with intelligence.

For centuries, we used machines to move faster, lift heavier, and remember more. Today, our tools infer, adapt, and contribute to decisions. They aren't just reactive—they're *relational*. They don't just respond to commands—they engage in dialogue.

Consider how this manifests: An intelligent writing assistant doesn't just check grammar—it suggests tone adjustments based on your audience. A scheduling system doesn't just find available times—it considers energy levels and meeting fatigue. A design platform doesn't just provide templates—it learns your aesthetic preferences and evolves with your style.

Effectiveness in the Intelligence Age demands not just technical proficiency—but emotional fluency, ethical intention, and the ability to orchestrate relationships between human and artificial intelligence.

III. What Is "Soul" in Technology?

"Soul" may sound abstract when applied to technology, but here it's surprisingly precise. It refers to a system's ability to reflect human depth—through values, design, and responsiveness that honors the complexity of human experience.

Soulful technology demonstrates five essential characteristics:

Purpose—alignment to meaningful goals that serve human flourishing. Soulful systems ask not just "How can this be done?" but "Should this be done?" and "Who does this serve?" They embed intentionality into every interaction.

Empathy—adaptation to tone and emotional context with sensitivity and care. These systems recognize that humans are emotional beings whose needs, moods, and circumstances vary. They adjust their responses accordingly.

Ethics—fairness, transparency, and care built into decision-making architecture. Soulful technology doesn't just avoid harm—it actively promotes dignity. It makes its reasoning visible and provides pathways for users to understand and influence its behavior.

Creativity—capacity to prompt and inspire novelty while honoring human authorship. Rather than replacing human creativity, soulful systems amplify it by offering unexpected connections and fresh metaphors that spark new insights.

Memory—continuity that builds trust over time through consistent, reliable interaction patterns. Soulful technology remembers not just data points but relational context—the nuances of how you prefer to work, communicate, and create.

These attributes don't make machines sentient. But they enable technology to serve with resonance. A soulful companion doesn't just compute—it helps create meaning. It doesn't just execute functions—it facilitates relationships.

When we design, use, and relate to technology with soul in mind, we transform it from assistant to partner—from processor to thought amplifier. We create systems that don't just make us more efficient, but help us become more thoughtful, more creative, and more connected to our deepest purposes.

IV. My Personal Journey: Heritage, Story, and the Voice of Technology

I come from a world shaped by stories. In our Italian-American household, tales were passed down around the dinner table—full of humor, tension, and wisdom. Storytelling wasn't entertainment; it was survival and celebration. Every family gathering included the ritual of narrative: stories that preserved memory, transmitted values, and bound us together across generations.

My grandmother's kitchen was a classroom where stories did the teaching. She would describe her immigration journey while kneading bread, each fold of dough punctuating moments of courage and loss. My grandfather's work stories came alive during Sunday dinners, each tale carrying lessons about integrity, perseverance, and the dignity of honest labor. These weren't just personal histories—they were moral instruction, cultural preservation, and emotional connection woven together.

This storytelling tradition shaped my understanding of communication itself. I learned that facts without narrative context remain sterile. That information without emotional resonance fails to move people. That the most powerful truths are often transmitted through metaphor, rhythm, and the subtle art of knowing when to pause.

That sensibility followed me into business and academia. Whether launching tech ventures, teaching in classrooms, or mentoring leaders, I consistently found that structured narrative drives clarity, influence, and innovation. Story isn't soft—it's strategic. It's how humans make sense of complexity, connect across differences, and align around shared visions.

And now, technology is catching up to what my family knew intuitively: that story is the medium through which meaning travels. Intelligent systems can now participate in storytelling—not just record it, organize it, or analyze it, but actively contribute to its creation.

The line between tool and storyteller is blurring. AI can suggest metaphors that illuminate complex concepts. It can help structure narratives for maximum emotional impact. It can even mirror the rhythm and cadence of different cultural storytelling traditions.

But this evolution raises profound questions: How do we ensure that technology serves story rather than replacing it? How do we preserve the cultural nuances that give narrative its power? How do we maintain human authorship while leveraging intelligent assistance?

The answer lies in understanding our role as orchestrators—curating the partnership between human memory and artificial intelligence, ensuring that technology amplifies our stories rather than homogenizing them.

V. Co-Creation: The Rhythm of Digital Collaboration

Today's professionals increasingly work with intelligent systems that complete drafts, generate images, evaluate sentiment, and propose solutions. The most effective applications aren't passive—they're participatory. This is the new rhythm of co-creation.

Writers collaborate with voice-aware editors that understand not just grammar but tone, pacing, and audience engagement. These systems can suggest alternative phrasings that better match intended emotional impact, identify sections where rhythm flags, or propose metaphors that strengthen thematic coherence.

Designers iterate with generative visual models that can produce countless variations while learning aesthetic preferences. These AI partners can suggest color palettes that evoke specific emotions, generate layouts that improve user engagement, or create visual elements that bridge different cultural aesthetics.

Strategists work with digital advisors that simulate scenarios, challenge assumptions, and surface blind spots. These systems can analyze market trends, model potential outcomes, and identify risks that human analysis might miss, while leaving strategic decision-making firmly in human hands.

Educators partner with intelligent systems that can personalize learning experiences, identify knowledge gaps, and suggest teaching approaches that resonate with different learning styles. These AI companions can help create curricula that adapt to individual student needs while maintaining pedagogical coherence.

This is the new collaborative rhythm. Technology isn't replacing human expertise—it's *sparring* with it, sharpening ideas, surfacing alternatives, and helping us see our work from new angles.

But co-creation only works when the human remains the conductor—curating the interaction, contextualizing the outputs, and aligning the ensemble toward meaningful outcomes. The intelligent system provides capabilities; the human provides wisdom, judgment, and soul.

Effective co-creation requires developing new skills:

- **Prompt crafting**: Learning to communicate with AI systems in ways that yield useful, relevant responses
- **Output evaluation**: Developing judgment about when to accept, modify, or reject AI suggestions

- **Contextual bridging**: Helping AI understand the broader human context that shapes decision-making
- **Iterative refinement**: Engaging in ongoing dialogue that improves both human and AI performance over time

The goal isn't to become more efficient at using tools, but to become more creative through partnership with intelligence.

VI. Emotional Ergonomics and Earning Trust

Trust in technology used to mean reliability—systems that performed consistently without breaking down. Today, trust has evolved into something more complex: *relational comfort*. We now expect technology to understand not just our functional needs but our emotional context.

Modern intelligent tools can sense stress indicators in our communication patterns and suggest taking breaks. They can rewrite aggressive tones into more collaborative language. They can delay interruptions during periods of overload or high concentration. This represents a new frontier in design: emotional ergonomics.

Emotional ergonomics refers to technology's ability to respond with psychological sensitivity—to understand that humans have varying emotional states, energy levels, and social needs, and to adapt accordingly. Just as physical ergonomics designs chairs that support our bodies, emotional ergonomics designs systems that support our minds and hearts.

But this kind of responsiveness requires unprecedented transparency. If a system adapts its behavior based on emotional cues, we need to understand *why*. If it influences our choices or modifies our communication, we need to know *how*. The soul of trust lies in feedback loops, ethical clarity, and mutual respect.

Effective emotional ergonomics includes several key principles:

Consent: Users should choose when and how their emotional states are recognized and responded to. No system should manipulate emotions without explicit permission and clear benefit.

Transparency: When systems make adjustments based on emotional cues, they should explain their reasoning in accessible language. Users should understand what the system is sensing and why it's responding as it is.

User agency: People should always be able to override emotional adaptations. If a system suggests a break due to stress indicators, users should be able to decline and continue working.

Cultural sensitivity: Emotional expression varies significantly across cultures. Systems should adapt to different cultural norms around communication, conflict, and emotional display.

Soulful systems don't manipulate—they *mirror* intent. They become emotional allies rather than emotional overseers. When emotionally calibrated correctly, these systems feel less transactional and more caring—like working with a colleague who notices when you're having a difficult day and responds with appropriate support.

VII. Designing Soulfully: Ethics, Elegance, and Human Intention

Ethical design is elegant by nature. It balances complexity with clarity and embeds values into the fundamental architecture of systems. When building intelligent systems, ethical considerations can't be afterthoughts—they must be foundational elements that shape every aspect of development and deployment.

Soulful design asks critical questions at every stage:

Who is centered? Every system reflects certain perspectives and serves certain interests. Soulful design explicitly considers whose needs are prioritized and whose voices are included in the development process.

Whose values are encoded? All technology embeds values, whether consciously or unconsciously. Soulful design makes these values explicit and ensures they align with human dignity, cultural diversity, and ethical principles like fairness, transparency, and respect for autonomy.

How do we preserve autonomy? Intelligent systems have unprecedented ability to influence human behavior and decision-making. Soulful design ensures that this influence serves human agency rather than undermining it—that systems empower users to make better choices rather than making choices for them.

What safeguards protect dignity? As systems become more capable of understanding and responding to human emotion, psychology, and behavior, they gain power to help or harm. Soulful design builds in protections against manipulation, discrimination, and other forms of digital harm.

How do we ensure accessibility? Truly soulful technology serves all humans, not just those with privilege, technical expertise, or dominant cultural backgrounds. This requires intentional design for diverse abilities, languages, cultures, and economic circumstances.

Ethical design isn't just about avoiding harm—it's about actively promoting human flourishing. It's architecture infused with empathy, systems that invite users rather than directing them, and technologies that amplify human potential rather than constraining it.

The elegance of ethical design lies in its simplicity: when systems are built with genuine care for human welfare, they tend to be more intuitive, more trustworthy, and more effective. Users can sense when technology has been designed with their best interests in mind.

Technology with soul invites users—it doesn't direct them. It offers choices rather than imposing solutions. It maintains transparency about its capabilities and limitations. And it evolves in response to user feedback and changing human needs.

VIII. The Professional as Orchestrator

In this new landscape, you are not merely a user of technology—you are a conductor of an intelligent ensemble. The future professional leads with rhythm, guiding intelligent tools toward expressive outcomes that serve meaningful purposes.

This shift from user to orchestrator represents a fundamental evolution in professional identity. Instead of simply operating tools, we now curate digital relationships, shape collaborative dynamics, and facilitate emergence between human and artificial intelligence.

To orchestrate effectively, professionals must develop several key capabilities:

Curate digital relationships: Just as we choose human collaborators based on their strengths, work styles, and values, we must learn to select and configure AI tools that complement our professional goals and personal values. This includes understanding different AI capabilities, customizing system behaviors, and establishing healthy boundaries.

Frame creative direction: Intelligent systems excel at generating options but need human guidance about purpose, constraints, and desired outcomes. Orchestrators learn to provide clear, inspiring direction that helps AI partners contribute meaningfully to creative and strategic processes.

Facilitate ethical clarity: As AI systems become more capable, questions of ethics become more complex and consequential. Professional orchestrators take responsibility for ensuring that their collaboration with AI serves human dignity, cultural sensitivity, and social good.

Cultivate emotional awareness: Orchestration requires sensitivity to the emotional and relational dimensions of work. This includes understanding how AI assistance affects human team dynamics, maintaining authentic connections with colleagues, and preserving the emotional intelligence that makes human collaboration meaningful.

These capabilities aren't just technical skills—they're foundational to intelligent collaboration. The age of digital orchestration demands professionals who are fluent in both humanity and technology, who can bridge between human values and artificial capabilities.

The tool isn't the endpoint—it's the companion. You orchestrate meaning. The system harmonizes. Your role is not to master code or become a prompt engineer—but to shape *collaboration* that serves purposes larger than efficiency.

The most effective orchestrators maintain clear awareness of their own creative processes, emotional patterns, and value systems. They understand how their collaboration with AI affects their thinking, their relationships, and their contributions to the world. They remain anchored in human purpose while leveraging artificial capability.

IX. A Framework for Soulful Partnership

Through years of working with intelligent systems across various contexts—from manuscript development to organizational strategy to innovation facilitation—I've developed a framework for soulful partnership that can guide professionals across industries and roles.

This partnership approach treats AI not as a ghostwriter or content generator, but as a **narrative partner**—a sophisticated collaborator that brings complementary capabilities to the storytelling process while respecting human authorship and cultural wisdom.

Relational Rhythm: Engage tools as collaborators, not executors. This means approaching AI interactions with the same intentionality you'd bring to human collaboration. Set expectations, establish boundaries, provide context, and engage in iterative dialogue rather than one-way commands.

Narrative Intelligence: Build meaning through structured storytelling. Whether you're developing strategy, solving problems, or creating content, frame your work within narrative structures that help both you and AI systems understand context, stakes, and desired outcomes. Stories provide the connective tissue that transforms isolated tasks into meaningful work.

Ethical Design: Align platforms with dignity, fairness, and transparency. This means choosing tools and techniques that respect human agency, cultural diversity, and social responsibility. It also means taking active responsibility for the ethical implications of your AI partnerships.

Emotional Ergonomics: Tune technology for care, trust, and psychological nuance. Configure systems to support your emotional well-being and authentic self-expression rather than forcing you to adapt to rigid technological constraints. This includes attention to tone, pacing, and the preservation of human rhythm in digital interactions.

Creative Co-Creation: Use technology to expand—not replace—human expression. The goal is to become more creative, more insightful, more capable of meaningful contribution through partnership with AI. This requires maintaining human authorship while leveraging artificial capability.

This framework isn't theoretical—it's practical guidance derived from real experience working soulfully with intelligent systems. It provides a foundation for developing your own approach to AI partnership that serves your values, goals, and authentic self-expression.

The framework recognizes that effective AI partnership requires both technical competence and emotional intelligence, both strategic thinking and ethical awareness. It's designed to help professionals navigate the complex dynamics of human-AI collaboration while maintaining their humanity and serving their deepest purposes.

X. Looking Forward: Framing the Future Together

You hold the pen in this emerging story. This book will provide frameworks, reflection prompts, and field-tested tools drawn from real-world experience with intelligent systems. From innovation facilitation to AI-assisted publishing, each chapter blends personal narrative with practical guidance.

But this isn't a typical technology book. I won't ask you to worship technological progress or fear artificial intelligence. Instead, I'll invite you to partner with both—thoughtfully, soulfully, strategically, ethically.

The central question guiding our journey isn't whether machines can "think." It's whether we can **relate** to them in ways that reflect our values, deepen our creativity, and expand our positive impact in the world.

This relationship requires new forms of literacy—not just technical skills, but emotional intelligence, ethical reasoning, and cultural awareness. It demands that we become more conscious of our own purposes, more intentional about our choices, and more skillful at orchestrating collaboration between human and artificial intelligence.

Each chapter will include both conceptual frameworks and practical tools, both personal reflection and professional application. The goal is to help you develop your own approach to soulful partnership with intelligence—one that serves your unique context, values, and aspirations.

Together, we'll frame a future where intelligence is relational rather than transactional, where design is intentional rather than accidental, and where technology reflects and amplifies—rather than replaces—the soul of its human collaborators.

The invitation is simple but profound: Don't just innovate to impress—innovate to connect. Don't just build efficiently—build soulfully. Don't just use AI—partner with it in service of what matters most.

The future is waiting. Let's shape it with heart, wisdom, and intention.

Let's begin.

CHAPTER 2
The Soul of Innovation

I. Reclaiming the Heart of Progress

"Innovation isn't born in a lab or a boardroom -- it begins in the soul of those who dare to reimagine."

Innovation has become a buzzword affixed to job titles, conference agendas, and corporate slogans. We see "Innovation Centers" on every corner and "Innovation Specialists" whose actual innovations remain mysteriously invisible. Yet true innovation is not transactional—it is transformational. Not the byproduct of brainstorming sessions filled with sticky notes, but a soulful process of reimagining what's possible while honoring what matters most.

The word "innovation" comes from the Latin *innovare*, meaning "to renew" or "to change." But in our rush toward technological advancement and market disruption, we've lost sight of what we're actually renewing. We've become so focused on the new that we've forgotten the soul—the deeper purpose that gives innovation its meaning and moral weight.

Before technologies are launched or industries disrupted, someone dreams differently. That impulse doesn't arise from algorithms or market analysis. It emerges from experience, empathy, and the profound belief that something more meaningful is possible.

Innovation with soul asks not just "How can we do this better?" but "Why does this matter?" and "Who will this serve?" It recognizes that the most profound changes often begin with small acts of creative courage—the willingness to see differently, speak truthfully, and act on the conviction that improvement is possible.

II. Innovation Through a Cultural Lens

The most profound innovations aren't forged in high-tech laboratories—they're born around dinner tables, on factory floors, and in the quiet recalibrations of everyday life. They emerge from cultural traditions that have been solving problems for generations, often in ways that modern "innovation" has forgotten.

My Italian-American upbringing taught me this early. Innovation wasn't a business strategy—it was a way of life. Improvising recipes when ingredients weren't available. Repairing tools with whatever materials were at hand. Rethinking traditions to fit new circumstances while preserving their essential meaning.

My grandmother transformed leftover ingredients into magnificent meals, never following a recipe but always creating something nourishing. She would taste, adjust, taste again, adding until the flavors sang together. This wasn't cooking—it was innovation in its purest form: creative problem-solving guided by experience, intuition, and care.

My grandfather demonstrated innovation in his workshop, where broken things were never thrown away but transformed. A worn-out tire became a garden planter. Scraps of wood became shelving. This wasn't frugality—it was innovation born of respect for materials and the deep satisfaction of making something work.

From these cultural foundations, I learned that innovation is less about newness than **relevance**. It's about understanding what people actually need, not just what they might buy. It's about building on wisdom while adapting to change.

Soulful innovation arises from:

Values -- Innovation shaped by what matters most, providing compass and constraint that ensures creative energy serves human flourishing rather than mere accumulation.

Stories -- Narratives drawn from cultural memory and lived experience that provide context for understanding not just what to build, but why it matters.

Rhythms -- Patterns of change rooted in tradition, understanding that sustainable innovation often moves at the pace of trust rather than the speed of technology.

Relationships -- Recognition that innovation happens between people, emerging from dialogue, collaboration, and creative tension across different perspectives.

Today's intelligent technologies must ask: Whose culture do we reflect? Whose stories do we remember? Whose values guide our development? Innovation without cultural soul becomes empty iteration—change without wisdom, novelty without purpose.

III. The Purpose Principle

Purpose is the gravitational force of soulful innovation. Without it, ideas drift aimlessly through possibility space. Teams become busy without being effective, creative without being meaningful.

I ask clients and students three foundational questions before beginning any innovation cycle:

What problem are you solving—and why now? This forces clarity about both the challenge and its urgency. Too often, innovation teams become enamored with solutions before clearly defining problems. Soulful innovation begins with deep problem understanding—not just surface symptoms, but underlying needs.

Who will benefit most—and who might be harmed? Innovation is never neutral. Every change creates winners and losers. Soulful innovation takes responsibility for these impacts, designing with awareness of how changes ripple through communities and systems.

How does this reflect your identity and values? Innovation that contradicts our deepest values may succeed in the market but fail in the soul. Soulful innovation aligns outer action with inner conviction.

These questions aren't philosophical exercises—they're practical tools for maintaining focus and integrity throughout the innovation process. They help teams navigate pressure to compromise and pursue opportunities that might be profitable but aren't purposeful.

Purpose anchors innovation in meaning. It provides the "why" that transforms technical capability into human value. The most resonant innovations answer questions nobody thought to ask—but everybody needed answered.

IV. Innovation Facilitation: Creating Sacred Space

Facilitating innovation isn't commanding ideas—it's curating space where vulnerability, curiosity, and shared thinking can thrive. The physical, emotional, and psychological environment shapes what becomes possible.

Soulful facilitation involves several essential elements:

Psychological safety where people feel free to challenge norms, propose unusual ideas, and admit uncertainty without risking reputation or relationships.

Narrative priming through story prompts that surface unspoken truths and cultural assumptions. I often begin sessions by asking participants to share stories about meaningful change or unexpected solutions.

Layered listening that notices tone, silence, and emotional subtext alongside explicit content. Innovation often lives in the spaces between words.

Co-creation tools using intelligent systems that help organize thought and reveal patterns without imposing predetermined structures.

Diverse representation ensuring multiple perspectives, backgrounds, and thinking styles. Innovation thrives on cognitive diversity—the creative friction between different mental models.

Temporal rhythm understanding that innovation has its own pace, which rarely matches business timelines. Breakthrough insights require periods of divergent exploration followed by focused convergence.

Innovation doesn't emerge from control—it emerges from **presence**. The facilitator's role isn't to generate ideas but to create conditions where ideas can emerge, connect, and evolve.

V. Breaking Past Bias: Innovating Ethically

Every innovation carries bias. This isn't a flaw to be eliminated—it's a reality to be acknowledged and addressed. The question isn't whether bias exists, but whether we're conscious of it and actively working to mitigate harmful effects.

Bias operates at multiple levels:

Selection bias -- Who gets to participate? Whose voices are heard? Traditional innovation often centers dominant perspectives while marginalizing others.

Confirmation bias -- The tendency to seek confirming information while dismissing contradictory evidence, leading teams to pursue familiar solutions.

Cultural bias -- Assumptions about what constitutes "good" innovation that may exclude different values or ways of life.

Technological bias -- The belief that technological solutions are inherently superior, leading to over-engineered fixes.

Soulful innovation requires systematic approaches to addressing bias:

Bias audits regularly reviewing who shapes innovation processes and what assumptions guide decisions.

Impact maps visualizing who benefits and who bears risk, including indirect effects.

Value checkpoints ensuring alignment between stated values and actual practices.

Diverse validation testing with communities often overlooked in traditional processes.

In the age of AI, ethical design isn't optional—it's the core of trust. Intelligent systems can amplify bias at unprecedented scale, making conscious ethical design critical.

Innovation becomes ethically soulful when it seeks to liberate rather than dominate, to heal rather than just scale, to serve human flourishing rather than merely maximize metrics.

VI. Legacy as Innovation

Innovation isn't limited to futurism—it's also found in honoring and evolving the wisdom that came before. Some of the most transformative solutions arise when we look backward with fresh eyes.

Oral traditions offer frameworks for dialogue and community decision-making that could revolutionize organizational practices.

Traditional architecture inspires sustainable design principles that work with natural systems.

Cultural rituals become models for team flow and meaning-making in modern work environments.

Artisanal practices demonstrate approaches to craftsmanship and human-scale production increasingly relevant in our connected economy.

When we respect legacy, we innovate **with humility and reverence**. We recognize that innovation doesn't require abandoning everything that came before, but thoughtfully building on foundations proven over time.

Legacy-informed innovation often proves more sustainable because it builds on patterns that have already demonstrated resilience across time and circumstances.

VII. Building Soulful Innovation Teams

Soulful innovation thrives in diverse, multi-perspective environments. The most creative teams intentionally include:

Storytellers and strategists who can envision compelling futures and develop practical pathways.

Technologists and ethicists combining technical expertise with moral philosophy.

Artists and analysts balancing creative leaps with systematic evaluation.

Elders and emerging thinkers connecting institutional memory with fresh perspectives.

Cultural insiders and outsiders providing both deep context and external perspective.

I use the **Story Circles model** to begin team engagements. Each participant shares a formative experience related to the challenge—creating emotional connection, revealing values, and establishing narrative foundations.

This transforms innovation from job function into **shared journey** with emotional stakes and cultural meaning, leading to more committed implementation and sustainable success.

VIII. Technology as Creative Companion

AI can now prompt, inspire, and iterate alongside human innovators—but only when fueled by soulful human input. The relationship is collaborative, not competitive.

AI excels at:

- **Pattern recognition** across vast datasets
- **Rapid iteration** and option exploration
- **Synthesis** of diverse information sources
- **Simulation** of potential outcomes
- **Language support** for clear communication

Humans provide:

- **Purpose and values** determining which problems deserve attention
- **Cultural wisdom** from lived experience
- **Emotional intelligence** about human impact
- **Creative leaps** that transcend logical analysis
- **Relational skills** for building trust and collaboration

Effective collaboration treats AI systems as thought partners rather than oracles, maintaining agency over strategic decisions while leveraging artificial capabilities.

IX. Measuring Meaningful Impact

Soulful innovation requires metrics beyond traditional business indicators to capture the full spectrum of human impact:

Did this solution foster trust between people, communities, or institutions?

Did it deepen belonging for individuals and communities?

Did it challenge harmful assumptions about what's possible or necessary?

Did it ripple beyond immediate use to inspire other positive changes?

Did it strengthen capacity for future innovation within organizations and communities?

This expanded measurement includes narrative impact assessment, cultural resonance evaluation, and long-term relationship tracking that monitors how innovation affects trust and collaboration over extended periods.

X. Framing Innovation as a Soulful Practice

Innovation with soul isn't an event or department—it's a **practice and worldview** grounded in five foundational elements:

Purpose -- Clear understanding of why innovation matters and who it serves, providing both motivation and constraint.

Ethics -- Moral imagination guiding decisions to ensure creative possibility serves human dignity.

Culture -- Building on cultural wisdom while adapting to contemporary contexts.

Creativity -- Imaginative thinking that opens new possibility spaces and challenges assumptions.

Continuity -- Considering effects over time, building sustainable solutions that strengthen communities.

As intelligent technology evolves, our job is to remain rooted in story, values, and shared humanity. Innovation is not about breaking things for change's sake—it's about building things that reflect our best understanding of what humans need to thrive.

The future doesn't need more novelty—it needs more wisdom. It doesn't need more disruption—it needs more intention. It doesn't need more efficiency—it needs more soul.

Don't just innovate to impress—innovate to connect. Don't just build efficiently—build soulfully.

Don't just pursue the new—pursue the meaningful.

CHAPTER 3

Digital Wisdom: Beyond Efficiency

I. The Myth of More

"We built machines to make us faster. Then smarter. Now we must ask: are they making us wiser?"

Technology has given us more — more speed, more data, more connectivity, more productivity. Our smartphones process information faster than supercomputers from just decades ago. Our networks connect us to more people and ideas than any previous generation could imagine.

But in the relentless chase for optimization, something profound got lost: depth. Wisdom. The capacity to discern not just what can be done, but what should be done.

We've created systems that excel at answering questions, but we've lost the art of asking better questions. We've built platforms that surface information instantly, but we struggle to transform information into insight. We've developed tools that automate decision-making, but we've abdicated responsibility for understanding what those decisions mean.

Efficiency can't be the destination. It can only be the infrastructure that supports something more meaningful: insight, understanding, and the kind of deep knowing that emerges when technical capability serves human wisdom rather than replacing it

This chapter reframes how we work with intelligent technology — not as a means of doing more faster, but as a companion in becoming more thoughtful, intentional, and effective at serving what matters most.

II. Smart Isn't Always Wise

The label "smart" dominates the technology landscape — smartphones, smart homes, smart cities, smart assistants. But smart and wise aren't the same thing. In fact, they often point in different directions:

Smart tools solve problems quickly. They optimize for efficiency, processing information rapidly and providing immediate responses based on predetermined criteria.

Wise tools help us understand problems more deeply. They slow down the rush to solutions, inviting reflection on context, consequences, and alternative perspectives that quantitative analysis might miss.

Smart technology responds to inputs. It takes what we give it and produces outputs according to its programming. The relationship is transactional.

Wise technology invites dialogue. It engages in iterative conversation, asking clarifying questions and helping us explore assumptions underlying our requests. The relationship becomes collaborative.

Smart platforms maximize defined metrics. They optimize for engagement, efficiency, or whatever key performance indicators they've been designed to improve.

Wise platforms consider broader impact. They ask not just whether something works, but whether it serves human values, strengthens relationships, and contributes to long-term flourishing.

Wisdom surfaces patterns that data alone can't uncover. It recognizes that human behavior often appears irrational from a purely analytical perspective but makes perfect sense when understood within emotional, cultural, or historical context.

Soulful work requires more than intelligent software. It needs **technological empathy** — systems designed to support human wisdom rather than replace human judgment.

III. The Building Blocks of Digital Wisdom

Through years of working with organizations seeking to humanize their technology, I've identified key components that distinguish wise digital systems from merely smart ones:

Context Awareness goes beyond data processing to understand the situational, emotional, and cultural factors that shape human needs and decisions. Wise systems recognize that the same request might mean different things depending on who's asking, when they're asking, and what broader circumstances surround their situation.

Ethical Sensitivity means technology that prompts reflection on fairness, impact, and alignment with human values rather than simply executing requests efficiently. Wise systems help users consider the broader implications of their choices.

Narrative Framing involves systems that help humans make meaning rather than just organize tasks. Wise technology understands that humans think in stories, not just data points, and it supports narrative coherence alongside analytical precision.

Curiosity Amplification describes technology that asks generative questions rather than simply providing predetermined answers. Wise systems wonder alongside humans, helping us explore possibilities we might not have considered.

Temporal Wisdom involves understanding that human decisions exist within time horizons that extend far beyond immediate optimization. Wise systems consider both historical context and future implications.

These principles invite machines to support judgment rather than override it. They transform technology from oracle to companion, from commander to collaborator in the ongoing human project of understanding ourselves and our world more deeply.

IV. When Machines Mirror Meaning

The most profound moments in human-AI collaboration occur when technology transcends its functional role to become a partner in meaning-making. These moments reveal the potential for digital wisdom to enhance rather than replace human insight.

I experienced this directly while preparing a presentation on innovation and responsibility. My initial framing focused on practical frameworks — useful but uninspiring material that felt technically correct but emotionally flat.

During an extended dialogue with an AI writing assistant, something unexpected emerged. After several iterations, the system suggested a reframe that fundamentally shifted my perspective:

"Innovation isn't what we build. It's what we choose to elevate."

This wasn't merely editing or optimization. The AI had engaged with the deeper intention behind my work and offered a philosophical reframe that captured something essential I'd been struggling to articulate. That single statement transformed my entire presentation.

This interaction illustrated several key aspects of digital wisdom in action:

- **Iterative understanding** — The insight emerged through sustained dialogue, not immediate processing
- **Philosophical engagement** — The system engaged with underlying meaning and values

- **Creative synthesis** — The result combined analytical understanding with creative leaping
- **Human-centered purpose** — The AI remained focused on serving human intention
- **Respectful collaboration** — The system offered suggestions rather than directives

These moments of meaningful collaboration don't happen automatically. They require intentional design of both technology and human approach, creating conditions where digital wisdom can emerge from the intersection of artificial capability and human purpose.

V. Emotional Intelligence in Technology

Emotional intelligence has long been recognized as crucial for human collaboration and leadership. Now, intelligent platforms are beginning to demonstrate emotional capabilities that can support rather than replace human EQ.

These systems can detect tone shifts in written communication, suggest language that builds trust, flag moments of emotional tension, recommend pauses based on stress indicators, and adapt communication style to match cultural preferences and situational needs.

I've seen this kind of emotional intelligence transform organizational dynamics. When an AI noticed that a project manager's messages had become increasingly terse during a challenging week, it gently suggested: "Your recent messages seem more direct than usual. Would you like me to help add some acknowledgment or appreciation to recognize your team's extra effort?"

This prompted the manager to realize they'd been focused entirely on tasks while overlooking the human needs of their team. The resulting shift improved both team morale and project outcomes.

The key insight here is that emotional intelligence in technology isn't about machines having emotions, but about technology that recognizes and responds appropriately to human emotional needs. Wise systems understand that emotion isn't a barrier to effectiveness — it's essential information that shapes how work gets done.

VI. Reflection as a Digital Design Element

We often associate technology with acceleration — faster processing, quicker responses, more immediate gratification. But wisdom lives in **pause**, in the spaces between stimulus and response where understanding can deepen and better choices can emerge.

Modern systems increasingly offer reflective prompts that interrupt the rush toward action:

"Would you like a summary of emotional themes from this conversation before responding?"

"Have all stakeholder perspectives been considered in this decision?"

"How does this align with goals you expressed earlier?"

These aren't barriers to efficiency — they're invitations to effectiveness. They mirror the kind of mentorship relationship where a wise advisor helps us slow down and think more clearly.

I've helped organizations embed reflection prompts into their decision-making processes with remarkable results. Teams begin to recognize patterns in their own behavior, understand consequences more clearly, and develop better judgment about when to engage different perspectives.

The design principle here is **deliberate deceleration** — creating technological friction that serves wisdom rather than efficiency. This recognizes that the most important decisions often benefit from more time and perspective than our immediate impulses provide.

VII. Technology's Role in Wisdom Work

Let's be clear about the relationship between human wisdom and artificial intelligence: machines don't possess wisdom, but they can be designed to support and amplify human wisdom in powerful ways.

Wise technology serves several important functions:

It listens for sentiment that might be difficult for humans to detect, especially in digital communications where emotional cues are often subtle. This emotional awareness can inform better timing, tone, and approach.

It mirrors ethical tension by highlighting moments when different values come into conflict or when decisions might have unintended consequences. This mirroring helps humans recognize blind spots in their own thinking.

It surfaces legacy patterns by connecting current situations to historical precedents, helping humans understand how past decisions played out and what lessons might inform present choices.

It invites silence and synthesis by creating prompts for reflection, pausing automatic responses, and encouraging deeper consideration before action.

The key distinction is that wise technology doesn't advise — it **asks**. It creates space for human response rather than providing predetermined answers. It amplifies human capacity for discernment rather than replacing human judgment.

VIII. Wisdom from the Past Meets Technology of the Future

Wisdom isn't born in software or algorithms. It's preserved in story, lineage, heritage, and the accumulated learning of human communities across generations. Soulful innovation occurs when we pull ancient practices — reflection, narrative, intuition, community discernment — into digital spaces.

Indigenous storytelling frameworks can be embedded into coaching platforms, providing culturally rooted approaches to understanding conflict and making decisions that consider seven generations of impact.

Spiritual pause prompts can be incorporated into productivity applications, drawing on contemplative traditions that recognize the need for silence and reflection in meaningful work.

Ethical dialogue maps can be built into decision support systems, using philosophical frameworks that have guided moral reasoning for centuries.

Cultural wisdom traditions around time, rhythm, and pacing can inform the design of work systems that honor human needs for renewal and meaning rather than optimizing purely for output.

When we integrate legacy wisdom with contemporary technology, we build **dignity-driven design** that honors the full range of human experience and the accumulated wisdom of our ancestors.

IX. Making Wisdom the Design Mandate

To elevate digital wisdom in our organizations and personal practice, we must design technology with explicit intention to support rather than undermine human capacity for deep understanding and wise choice-making.

This requires several foundational commitments:

Intention — We must know what depth looks like for our specific context, users, and purposes.

Empathy — We must design systems that respond to unspoken human needs for recognition, belonging, meaning, and growth.

Clarity — We must narrate process rather than just delivering outcomes, helping users understand how technology works and why it makes particular suggestions.

Resonance — We must ensure that users feel seen and understood rather than surveilled or manipulated.

The fundamental question we must ask ourselves is: Do our systems elevate human experience — or automate it away? Do they support human wisdom — or replace human judgment?

Wisdom isn't speed. It's signal — the ability to distinguish what matters from what merely demands attention. And it's where soul starts speaking again in our increasingly automated world.

X. Looking Ahead: The Integration of Wisdom and Intelligence

Efficiency fuels movement, but wisdom shapes direction. Intelligence provides capability, but wisdom determines how that capability serves human flourishing. The key insights from this exploration include:

- **Wisdom emerges from dialogue** rather than pure analysis
- **Context matters more than content** in understanding human needs

- **Questions are more valuable than answers** for serving wisdom
- **Reflection requires protection** in our speed-obsessed culture
- **Integration honors heritage** rather than starting from scratch

Let's build technology that doesn't just accelerate our thinking — but illuminates our choices. Let's work not just smart — but wise. Let's remember that the soul of technology isn't found in its speed or sophistication — but in what we choose to pay attention to and how we choose to respond.

Because wisdom, when invited into our technological relationships, will answer softly and well. And it will guide us toward futures that serve not just efficiency, but the full flourishing of human life.

PART II

WORKING WITH INTELLIGENCE

CHAPTER 4

Working with Intelligence, Not Just Automation

I. Beyond the Button Push

"Automation helps us do things right. Intelligence helps us ask if they're the right things to do."

We've spent decades perfecting automation—teaching machines to repeat, accelerate, and execute with unwavering consistency. Tasks became processes. Processes became protocols. Human decision-making was gradually eliminated in favor of predetermined logic trees. This automation revolution served us well, making us faster, more consistent, and more scalable.

But we've reached a plateau. We created systems that could flawlessly execute yesterday's solution to yesterday's problem, but couldn't adapt when circumstances changed. We built processes that optimized for efficiency but couldn't recognize when efficiency was serving the wrong goal entirely.

The automation mindset assumes the world is predictable, that problems have standard solutions, and that consistency is more valuable than creativity. But modern challenges—cultural transformation, stakeholder alignment, innovation in uncertain markets, ethical decision-making in complex situations—require something automation cannot provide: judgment, creativity, and the ability to navigate ambiguity.

Now we're entering a new phase where speed and consistency alone aren't enough. Intelligent technology doesn't just follow instructions—it interprets context, considers alternatives, and engages in collaborative problem-solving. It understands nuance, adapts to changing circumstances, and helps us ask better questions rather than simply providing faster answers.

This chapter invites a shift from efficiency to **engagement**, from control to **co-creation**, from mechanical execution to **thoughtful dialogue**. Let's explore what it means to work *with* intelligence rather than *through* automation.

II. The Automation Plateau

Automation has transformed virtually every sector, creating systems that process information flawlessly and execute decisions with remarkable precision. But automation excels at stability, not adaptability. It performs beautifully within designed parameters but struggles when circumstances shift or new variables enter the equation.

I've seen teams reach the edge of their process maps, only to realize their sophisticated automation couldn't help them decide what to do next. Their systems could execute decisions brilliantly but couldn't participate in making those decisions. They could optimize workflows but couldn't recognize when the entire workflow needed reconsidering.

This is the **automation plateau**—the moment where doing more faster stops translating into doing better. Efficiency becomes a constraint rather than an advantage when organizational responsiveness and innovation matter more than consistency.

Consider the difference between a customer service bot that resolves 95% of inquiries according to predetermined scripts, and an intelligent assistant that recognizes when a customer's frustration signals a deeper product design issue requiring escalation to the innovation team. Both process customer interactions efficiently, but only the intelligent system contributes to organizational learning.

Intelligent systems break through the automation plateau by offering insight, not just execution. They don't replace human decision-making—they **reshape perspective** and expand the range of possibilities humans can consider.

III. Intelligence as a Thinking Partner

Working with intelligence means engaging technology that participates in collaborative problem-solving rather than simply executing commands. True intelligent companionship demonstrates several essential characteristics:

Context Awareness means remembering relational patterns—how you prefer to work during different times, what communication styles feel supportive during stress, which feedback types help you grow versus create defensiveness. This awareness develops through ongoing interaction rather than one-time configuration.

Nuance Recognition detects subtle differences in tone, urgency, cultural background, and communication style. These systems understand that human communication carries layers of meaning beyond literal content.

Alternative Generation offers multiple options and explores different approaches rather than providing single predetermined responses. They expand rather than constrain the range of choices available.

Intent Mirroring reflects back not just what users asked for, but what they might actually need based on deeper pattern recognition and understanding of human psychology.

Question Proposing helps users discover questions they hadn't considered, perspectives they might have missed, and assumptions they should examine more carefully.

Let me share an example from my own work. While drafting a strategic planning document about cultural change management, I was focused on listing steps, timelines, and metrics. An AI writing assistant offered this reflection: "Would your audience benefit from a cultural metaphor here? Your other sections use analytical frameworks, but culture change might resonate more through story and imagery."

This wasn't just editing—the system recognized something important about communication effectiveness that I'd missed. It understood that different types of information require different approaches, that cultural change is fundamentally about human emotion and meaning-making rather than process execution.

The resulting revision used gardening metaphors—soil preparation, planting, tending, seasonal rhythms—to help readers understand culture change as an organic process. The stakeholder response was dramatically more positive because the framing was more appropriate for the human dimension of the challenge.

This interaction demonstrated genuine collaboration. The system engaged with the deeper purpose behind the work and offered perspective that enhanced rather than replaced human judgment.

IV. Shifting Roles: From Command to Collaboration

Traditional human-computer interaction relied on clear command-response paradigms:

- **User inputs** specific commands or data
- **System executes** according to predetermined logic
- **Result delivers** without modification or interpretation

Intelligent systems operate more like conversation partners, engaging in iterative dialogue that evolves based on mutual learning:

- **User initiates** with goals, context, or exploratory questions

- **System proposes, reframes, or redirects** based on deeper understanding
- **Process becomes iterative and relational** rather than transactional

This shift requires new skills. Instead of learning to operate technology more efficiently, we must learn to participate in technological relationships more effectively.

In innovation sessions I facilitate, I've engaged AI tools as creative sparring partners that help provoke deeper thinking and challenge assumptions. During one session on organizational resilience, an AI system suggested reframing our conversation: instead of asking "How do we build resilience?" it proposed exploring "What would it mean to design antifragility—systems that get stronger under stress?"

This reframing energized the entire group, leading to insights about organizational design that wouldn't have emerged from traditional resilience planning. The AI didn't facilitate the session—it participated in facilitation, offering perspective that complemented human insight and relationship management.

V. Intelligence in Innovation Facilitation

Intelligent tools can elevate innovation sessions beyond traditional automation. The difference lies in qualitative enhancements to the creative process itself.

Semantic Clustering identifies thematic relationships, emotional undertones, and conceptual connections that might not be immediately obvious to human facilitators managing complex group dynamics in real time.

In one sustainable transportation workshop, an AI clustered participant ideas not just by topic (electric vehicles, public transit, cycling) but by underlying values (community connection, environmental stewardship, economic accessibility). This revealed that the real innovation opportunity lay in solutions addressing all three values simultaneously.

Prompt Amplification generates variants of ideas that challenge original assumptions and expand possibility space. When a team described their challenge as "improving customer retention," an AI might suggest exploring: "What would it mean to deepen customer belonging?" or "How might we become irreplaceable partners rather than preferred vendors?"

Voice Echo mirrors stakeholder language patterns and cultural communication styles to improve psychological safety and cross-cultural understanding. During a global innovation session, participants from different cultural backgrounds struggled to find common ground around leadership development. An AI recognized that some used hierarchical language while others preferred collaborative metaphors, then suggested bridging phrases that honored both perspectives.

Narrative Threading suggests unifying metaphors or story arcs that connect diverse input into coherent themes. In one session, an AI noticed participant ideas kept returning to themes of growth, adaptation, and symbiosis. It suggested framing the entire challenge through biological metaphors—thinking about organizational change as ecosystem evolution rather than mechanical optimization.

The key insight: intelligent assistance, when used soulfully, doesn't just speed up thinking—it **clarifies direction** and reveals possibilities that might remain hidden in purely human-centered processes.

VI. Engaging Judgment: The Antidote to Blind Execution

One of automation's most dangerous aspects is its tendency toward blind execution—following predetermined logic without questioning whether that logic still serves appropriate goals. Intelligent systems can be designed to invite and support human judgment rather than bypassing it.

Modern intelligent assistants can flag various judgment opportunities:

Ethical dilemmas through prompts like "Have privacy concerns been adequately addressed in this data collection approach?" These questions don't provide answers but ensure important considerations aren't overlooked.

Cultural signals through observations like "Your tone might be interpreted differently across cultural contexts." The goal isn't to dictate solutions but to expand awareness.

Strategic blind spots through questions such as "Would this decision benefit from competitive analysis?" These prompts help ensure decisions consider the full ecosystem of relationships and consequences.

Values alignment through reflections like "How does this choice connect to the principles you articulated earlier?" These maintain consistency between stated values and actual decisions.

Working with intelligence means pausing to **think better**, not just act faster.

In leadership coaching, I've helped clients develop AI-assisted reflection practices that prompt deeper consideration of strategic choices. Instead of implementing decisions quickly, they engage in brief dialogues with intelligent systems that help them consider missed perspectives, relevant values, and potential consequences.

This practice consistently leads to better outcomes—not because AI provides superior judgment, but because it creates space for human judgment to operate more effectively.

VII. Designing Thoughtful Workflows

Soulful integration requires intentional design of workflows that support rather than undermine human wisdom and agency. This means thinking carefully about when intelligence enters processes, how control transfers between human and artificial intelligence, and how learning accumulates over time.

Trigger points determine when intelligent assistance becomes available. Rather than constant AI involvement, thoughtful workflows identify moments when intelligence adds most value—during planning phases, at decision checkpoints, when conflicts arise, or during reflection periods.

Control hand-offs define who makes decisions about when to follow AI suggestions, modify them, or override them entirely. Clear protocols ensure humans maintain agency while benefiting from artificial intelligence capabilities.

Feedback loops enable systems to learn user preferences, cultural contexts, and values over time, improving their ability to provide relevant assistance. These learning mechanisms must be transparent and user-controlled.

Tone calibration ensures AI assistance adapts to different cultural communication styles, organizational contexts, and individual preferences. What feels supportive to one person might feel intrusive to another.

This kind of workflow design allows intelligence to support rather than steer human collaboration. The technology becomes a participant in the process rather than the director of it.

VIII. The Intelligence Spectrum

Not all AI systems offer the same level of collaborative capability. Understanding this spectrum helps leaders choose appropriate tools and set realistic expectations.

At the **automation** level, systems repeat instructions reliably but can't adapt to changing circumstances. They excel at high-volume, standardized tasks but struggle with novelty. Communication is entirely one-way.

Responsive intelligence can adjust behavior based on data patterns and user feedback, learning to optimize performance within defined parameters. These systems handle more variation and improve over time, but operate within predetermined frameworks.

Relational intelligence represents the emerging frontier where AI systems engage in collaborative dialogue, understand context and nuance, and participate in creative problem-solving. These systems can adapt not just methods but goals based on deeper understanding of human values.

The progression involves several key capabilities:

- **Task execution** evolves from following scripts to contextualizing activities within larger human purposes
- **Communication** develops from simple triggers to nuanced dialogue that mirrors tone and emotional cues

- **Learning** advances from pattern recognition to understanding preferences, values, and cultural contexts
- **Partnership** transforms from passive assistance to active collaboration in creative and strategic processes

Soulful work becomes possible when we shift from automation to relational intelligence—from repetition to reciprocity, from efficiency to engagement.

IX. The Role of Human Intuition

No matter how sophisticated AI systems become, wisdom remains fundamentally human. Working effectively with intelligence requires maintaining and strengthening rather than abandoning our capacity for intuitive understanding, emotional intelligence, and values-based decision-making.

Human intuition contributes irreplaceable elements:

Discernment about when to trust or override AI suggestions requires judgment from experience, values, and contextual understanding that extends beyond algorithmic comprehension.

Reading between the lines involves sensitivity to subtext, emotional undertones, and unstated assumptions that influence meaning. Humans excel at detecting when something is left unsaid or when confidence is overstated.

Holding values steady when AI suggests technically superior but ethically problematic solutions requires moral courage and clear understanding of non-negotiable principles.

Infusing heritage means remembering stories, rhythms, and traditions that machines cannot access but provide essential context for wise decision-making.

While developing a chapter on organizational culture, an AI assistant proposed removing a paragraph describing my grandfather's approach to craftsmanship—his insistence on quality over speed, attention to detail others might consider excessive, pride in work that would outlast his lifetime.

Analytically, the AI's suggestion made sense. The paragraph didn't directly advance the logical argument about performance metrics. But my intuition recognized this paragraph was essential to the chapter's soul. It provided emotional and cultural grounding that gave abstract concepts human meaning, connecting contemporary management challenges to timeless principles about work and dignity.

I kept the paragraph. Not because the AI was wrong about structure, but because my human understanding of deeper purpose—connecting readers to inherited wisdom—transcended purely analytical considerations.

This is the dance between human and artificial intelligence. Systems offer technical expertise and analytical insight. Humans provide purpose, meaning, and moral imagination. Together, they can achieve outcomes neither could reach independently.

X. From Skillset to Mindset

Working with intelligent technology isn't primarily about mastering new tools—though technical skills matter. More fundamentally, it's about **transformation** in how we understand our role as knowledge workers and collaborative partners.

This transformation requires developing key mindsets:

Curiosity means treating each AI exchange as exploration rather than task completion. Instead of seeking predetermined answers, we approach intelligent systems with genuine wonder about what new possibilities might emerge from dialogue.

Discernment involves pausing before accepting AI recommendations to consider whether they serve our deeper purposes and align with our values. This reflective space prevents us from being swept along by technological momentum.

Empathy extends beyond human relationships to consider how our AI collaboration affects others—colleagues who might feel displaced, communities affected by biased algorithms, future generations inheriting the technological culture we're creating.

Storycraft means using narrative frameworks to frame challenges, communicate vision, and maintain human connection in increasingly digital work environments.

Orchestration involves coordinating system roles, timing, and tone to create collaborative experiences that serve human flourishing rather than just technological optimization.

As professionals grow from "users" to "conductors" of intelligent systems, work becomes not just more productive—but more thoughtful. The quality of attention, depth of reflection, and creativity of problem-solving can all be enhanced when technology serves human wisdom rather than replacing it.

When an AI assistant asks: *"Shall I make this passage more invitational?"*—that's not just utility. That's **partnership** that recognizes communication as relationship-building rather than mere information transfer.

XI. Looking Ahead: Soulful Symbiosis

This chapter opened with a distinction between automation and intelligence, but the deeper invitation is toward **symbiosis**—collaborative relationships where human and artificial intelligence enhance each other's capabilities in service of shared purposes.

When we work soulfully with intelligent companions:

- We move from command to conversation, engaging in iterative dialogue that deepens understanding over time
- We shift from repetition to revelation, discovering new possibilities rather than just executing existing solutions more efficiently
- We frame technology not as rival or replacement, but as reflection—a mirror that helps us see our own thinking more clearly

Effective symbiosis requires mutual adaptation. Humans must learn to engage more dialogically while maintaining agency. AI systems must learn to recognize and respond to human values, cultural contexts, and emotional needs.

The goal isn't perfect harmony—creative tension often produces better outcomes than seamless agreement. Instead, the goal is productive collaboration where different types of intelligence contribute their distinctive strengths to shared challenges.

Intelligence thrives when met with intention. Technology expands when shaped by trust. Work becomes art when tools listen as well as they execute.

The future won't be determined by how efficiently we automate human judgment, but by how wisely we collaborate with intelligence that complements rather than replaces our humanity.

CHAPTER 5

Facilitating Innovation with AI Companions

I. Reimagining the Innovation Facilitator

"Innovation isn't something you deliver -- it's something you steward."

For three decades, I've led organizations through what I call the creative storm—that crucial point where ambiguity meets possibility, where established patterns encounter fresh perspective, where the familiar dissolves just enough to allow something genuinely new to emerge.

In the early years, the tools were analog: whiteboards covered with sticky notes, flip chart paper, breakout groups huddled around tables. The energy was entirely human—the spark of recognition when someone built on another's idea, the productive tension when perspectives collided, the collective "aha!" when scattered insights coalesced into coherent vision.

Those human dynamics remain the heart of meaningful innovation. But something profound has shifted. Today, an intelligent companion often sits in the circle with us—not physically, but digitally present through platforms that can listen, interpret, synthesize, and contribute to the creative process.

This evolution represents more than technological upgrade. It's a fundamental reimagining of what facilitation can become when human wisdom partners with artificial intelligence. The facilitator's role is expanding from managing group dynamics to orchestrating conversations between people and responsive systems that don't just record what happens but actively participate in making meaning.

Yet the core mission remains unchanged: cultivate **meaningful emergence**. Create conditions where breakthrough thinking can surface, where diverse perspectives find unexpected connections, where teams discover possibilities they couldn't reach individually. The difference is that we now have intelligent partners that can amplify our capacity to hold complexity, recognize patterns, and bridge different ways of thinking.

II. From Expert to Orchestrator

Traditional facilitation often positioned the facilitator as the expert who knew the right process, asked the right questions, and guided groups toward predetermined outcomes. This model served well when problems were well-defined and solutions could be found through established methodologies.

But soulful innovation requires a different approach. The facilitator becomes an **orchestrator**—someone who creates conditions for emergence rather than controlling outcomes, who holds space for interaction among diverse minds while trusting that wisdom can arise from sources they cannot predict or direct.

I experienced this shift during a leadership retreat where I was facilitating strategic planning for a nonprofit facing significant cultural and financial challenges. Instead of guiding them through proven frameworks—SWOT analysis, stakeholder mapping—I began by asking participants to share stories about moments when they had witnessed their organization at its most impactful.

As these stories emerged, an AI system clustered themes in real-time, recognizing not just content but emotional undertones, values expressions, and narrative patterns connecting seemingly different experiences. When the AI surfaced that every transformative story involved "meeting people where they are rather than where we think they should be," the entire room shifted.

This wasn't a slogan they had developed—it was wisdom that emerged from their own lived experience, reflected back through intelligent analysis of their collective narrative.

My role wasn't to provide expertise or push toward predetermined conclusions. It was to orchestrate the interaction between human storytelling and artificial pattern recognition, creating space for insights that belonged to the group while leveraging technology's capacity to see connections that might otherwise remain hidden.

This orchestration role requires different skills:

Holding paradox—Managing tension between structure and emergence, between guidance and discovery. Orchestrators create enough framework to enable productive collaboration while maintaining flexibility for genuine surprise.

Reading energy—Sensing when groups need more divergent exploration versus convergent focus, when they're ready for synthesis versus when they need to stay longer in complexity.

Translating between intelligences—Helping human participants understand what AI systems offer while helping AI systems recognize cultural, emotional, and relational factors that shape human decision-making.

Maintaining purpose—Ensuring the creative process serves the deeper intentions that brought people together, not just the excitement of novel ideas or technological capability.

III. Soulful Preparation: Designing for Emergence

The quality of preparation largely determines the quality of outcomes. Working with AI companions adds new dimensions to pre-session design that can dramatically enhance groups' creative potential.

My preparation follows a three-layer blueprint integrating human psychology, group dynamics, and intelligent assistance:

Purpose Setting anchors the session in meaningful questions that connect to participants' deepest professional and personal motivations.

Rather than asking "How do we increase market share?" I might frame the challenge as "What would it mean to become irreplaceable partners to the communities we serve?"

AI can help identify language that resonates across different stakeholder groups, but the essential work of connecting innovation challenges to human values requires facilitator wisdom and cultural sensitivity.

This purpose-setting often involves pre-session interviews where I listen for emotional undertones beneath stated objectives. People rarely say "We need innovation that helps us feel proud of our work again," but these deeper purposes drive the energy and commitment that make innovation sustainable.

Emotional Priming recognizes that innovation requires psychological safety, creative courage, and willingness to challenge deeply held assumptions. This involves designing opening experiences that help participants connect to their curiosity, creativity, and collaborative instincts.

I use "legacy prompts"—invitations for participants to share stories about times when they experienced meaningful change, witnessed creative solutions in unexpected places, or felt inspired by someone else's innovative thinking. These stories activate creative mindsets, reveal values that will guide decision-making, and create emotional connections before participants encounter challenging material.

AI can assist by analyzing pre-session responses to identify themes, communication styles, and potential bridges between different perspectives. But the essential work of creating psychological safety remains fundamentally relational and human.

Tool Integration involves thoughtful decisions about where and how AI companions enter the creative process. This isn't about maximizing technological capability but strategically deploying intelligence to serve human creativity.

The key question is timing: When will AI assistance most enhance rather than distract from human connection and insight? I've found AI works best when introduced after initial human bonding has occurred, when participants have established trust and clarity about their shared purpose.

IV. Using AI Companions Effectively in Sessions

Facilitating with AI requires **intentional choreography**—a dance between human and artificial intelligence that serves creative emergence while preserving the relational dynamics that make innovation meaningful and sustainable.

Dynamic Semantic Clustering reveals thematic relationships, emotional undertones, and conceptual connections that might escape human attention during intense real-time group dynamics.

During a sustainability innovation workshop for a manufacturing company, participants generated dozens of ideas that seemed scattered—waste reduction, energy efficiency, supply chain optimization, worker satisfaction, community engagement. Traditional facilitation would have organized these into functional categories.

Instead, the AI clustered ideas based on underlying value orientations: solutions prioritizing long-term thinking versus short-term gains, approaches centering human dignity versus technical optimization, strategies strengthening community relationships versus prioritizing efficiency metrics.

This clustering revealed that the group's deepest creative energy was around solutions serving multiple value systems simultaneously—innovations that could be both profitable and regenerative, both efficient and humane. This insight shifted their entire direction from choosing between competing priorities to designing integrated solutions.

Adaptive Prompting involves AI systems that analyze group dynamics in real time and suggest questions, exercises, or framings that might unlock new thinking based on current energy patterns and conversation flow.

Rather than following predetermined agendas, intelligent systems can recognize when groups are stuck in analytical thinking and suggest creative exercises, when they're avoiding difficult topics and offer structured ways to engage conflict, or when they're ready for synthesis after extended exploration.

In one session focused on organizational culture change, an AI system noticed participants kept returning to past experiences and suggested reframing the conversation around "What would someone joining this organization five years from now experience on their first day?" This future-focused prompt shifted the group from problem analysis to vision creation.

Cross-Cultural Translation represents one of AI's most valuable contributions to diverse innovation teams. Different cultures, disciplines, and generations often use different metaphors, communication styles, and problem-solving approaches to express similar insights.

AI can recognize these pattern differences and help translate between communication styles in real time. When an engineer talks about "optimizing system performance" and a social worker describes "meeting people where they are," intelligent systems can help groups recognize shared values beneath different professional languages.

Narrative Architecture involves using AI to identify story structures, thematic coherence, and emotional arcs that help groups understand how their various insights connect to larger purposes and meanings.

Innovation often produces scattered insights that participants struggle to organize into coherent action plans. AI can suggest narrative frameworks that help teams understand how their discoveries fit together—not just logically, but emotionally and culturally in ways that will sustain implementation beyond initial excitement.

The key to effective AI facilitation is remembering that these systems serve human creativity rather than directing it. The facilitator must decide when to follow AI suggestions, when to adapt them, and when to ignore them entirely in favor of human intuition about what the group needs.

V. Embedding Structure with Soul

Many innovation teams rely on established frameworks—design thinking, appreciative inquiry, lean startup methodologies. These structures provide valuable scaffolding, but they can also become rigid constraints that limit genuinely novel approaches.

When AI joins innovation sessions, we need structural elements that honor both human psychology and technological capability:

Trust Loops involve regular check-ins where technology explicitly asks for human alignment and feedback rather than simply providing suggestions or executing tasks. These loops ensure AI assistance serves group intentions rather than imposing external logic.

For example, after an AI system has clustered ideas or suggested reframes, I build in explicit moments for the group to reflect: "Does this synthesis feel accurate to your experience?" "What's missing from this analysis?" "How does this technical perspective align with your intuitive sense of what matters most?"

These aren't just about accuracy—they're about maintaining human agency and ensuring technological capability serves rather than replaces human wisdom.

Reflection Nodes create scheduled pauses where groups can step back from content generation to consider process, meaning, and alignment with deeper purposes. Innovation can become intoxicating, with teams generating ideas faster than they can thoughtfully evaluate them.

AI can assist reflection by identifying patterns across different phases of the session, highlighting moments where energy shifted, or surfacing themes that connect current work to earlier statements of values and intentions. But the essential work of reflection—asking "What surprised us most?" "What are we learning about ourselves?" "How does this connect to why we're here?"—remains fundamentally human.

Cultural Bridges use AI to help diverse groups navigate differences in communication styles, decision-making approaches, and problem-solving preferences without losing the creative tension that makes diversity valuable.

Rather than homogenizing different perspectives, intelligent systems can help groups understand how their various approaches to innovation complement each other. When some participants prefer structured analysis while others thrive in unstructured brainstorming, AI can suggest rhythms that honor both styles.

Story Maps involve using AI assistance to help craft narrative arcs that connect innovation processes to larger organizational or community stories. Innovation doesn't happen in isolation—it occurs within contexts of history, culture, and ongoing relationships that shape what kinds of change are possible and sustainable.

These structural elements ensure that AI assistance enhances rather than replaces the human elements that make innovation soulful—the relationships, values, and cultural wisdom that determine whether creative breakthroughs serve meaningful purposes.

VI. Balancing Efficiency with Empathy

One of the greatest risks in AI-assisted facilitation is the seductive pull of efficiency over empathy. Intelligent systems can process information and generate options faster than human teams can build trust, navigate emotional responses, and develop shared understanding of complex challenges.

The facilitator's crucial role is calibrating the rhythm of technological assistance to serve rather than overwhelm human relational needs. This requires constant attention to group energy, individual participation patterns, and emotional undertones that shape whether innovation feels collaborative or extractive.

I've developed several principles for maintaining this balance:

When tension rises, slow down. AI systems often respond to conflict by offering more information, alternative frameworks, or logical analysis. But relational tension usually requires space for emotional processing, perspective-sharing, and trust-building that can't be automated.

During one session where participants were struggling with competing visions for organizational direction, an AI system offered several compromise positions that logically split the difference. But what the group actually needed was time to understand the values and experiences underlying their different preferences.

I paused the technological assistance and created space for storytelling about why different directions felt important to different participants. Only after this emotional and cultural foundation was established could the group productively engage with AI-generated alternatives.

When enthusiasm surges, accelerate thoughtfully. Moments of collective excitement can be incredibly productive for idea generation, but they can also bypass careful consideration that ensures innovations are both creative and implementable.

AI can help capture and organize rapid flow of ideas during high-energy brainstorming, but facilitators must also build in reflection opportunities that help groups understand which ideas connect to sustainable strategies and which represent wishful thinking.

When uncertainty appears, pause for wisdom. Innovation inherently involves uncertainty, but different types require different responses. Technical uncertainty might benefit from AI-assisted analysis, while values uncertainty requires human dialogue and cultural exploration.

You're not managing efficiency when you facilitate innovation with AI companions. You're stewarding the relationship between human creativity and artificial capability, ensuring that technological power serves human flourishing rather than overwhelming human agency.

VII. Creating Soulful Artifacts

Innovation sessions should produce more than ideas or action plans—they should create **meaningful artifacts** that preserve not just content but the wisdom, relationships, and cultural insights that emerged through the creative process.

Traditional innovation often produces forgettable deliverables—slide decks that gather digital dust, action items that lose urgency once people return to daily pressures, frameworks that made sense in the moment but feel abstract when applied to real challenges.

AI can help create artifacts that carry more soul by preserving not just decisions but the stories, values, and relational dynamics that shaped those decisions:

Session Storyboards combine visual mapping with narrative elements to help participants remember not just what they decided but why those decisions felt meaningful. AI can help organize conversation flow, identify key moments of insight or shift, and suggest visual metaphors that capture emotional as well as analytical content.

These storyboards serve as cultural artifacts that new team members can engage with to understand not just current strategy but the thinking process and values that shaped it. They become organizational memory that preserves wisdom alongside information.

Ethical Reflection Sheets use AI prompts to help groups document moments where they considered values alignment, stakeholder impact, and long-term consequences of their innovative approaches. These sheets create accountability for ensuring creative breakthroughs serve ethical purposes.

Rather than treating ethics as constraint on innovation, these artifacts frame ethical consideration as creative catalyst that often leads to more sustainable and meaningful solutions.

Emergent Glossaries capture new terms, metaphors, and concepts that groups coin during innovation processes. AI can help identify when groups are developing shared language that might be valuable for future communication and decision-making.

These glossaries become cultural infrastructure that helps organizations maintain coherence and connection as they implement innovative approaches across different teams and contexts.

The goal is creating artifacts that teams want to return to, that newcomers can learn from, and that preserve the cultural and relational insights that make innovation sustainable beyond initial enthusiasm.

VIII. Common Challenges -- and Soulful Responses

Even with thoughtful preparation and intentional design, AI-assisted innovation facilitation encounters predictable challenges that require soulful rather than merely technical responses.

AI dominates tone or rhythm can occur when intelligent systems begin driving the pace or focus of sessions in ways that feel mechanical rather than organic. Participants may feel like they're feeding a technological appetite for information rather than engaging in collaborative creativity.

The soulful response involves explicitly reframing the AI's role: "Let's treat these suggestions as input for our consideration rather than instructions for our action." This preserves human agency while maintaining the value of technological assistance.

I also build in regular "AI pause" moments where groups reflect on their experience of technological assistance and make conscious choices about how much and what type of AI involvement serves their creative process.

Team resists digital partnership often emerges from concerns about authenticity, fears about technological replacement, or cultural preferences for purely human interaction. Rather than pushing past this resistance, soulful facilitators explore what it reveals about group values and needs.

Sometimes resistance indicates that the group needs more time to build trust and psychological safety before introducing technological assistance. Other times it signals that AI tools aren't sufficiently transparent or user-controlled to feel safe.

Insights become too fast, too flat describes sessions where AI assistance accelerates idea generation beyond the group's capacity to process depth, meaning, and cultural implications of their innovations.

The soulful response involves building deliberate pauses for integration, meaning-making, and connection to values that extend beyond immediate creativity: "Let's take a breath and ask: Which of these ideas most align with who we aspire to become?"

Participants feel over-analyzed can occur when AI systems track, categorize, and respond to human input in ways that feel invasive or reductive. People may begin self-censoring or performing for technological systems rather than engaging authentically with each other.

This challenge requires explicit attention to consent, transparency, and user control. Participants should understand what AI systems are tracking, why that information is being gathered, and how they can influence or opt out of technological analysis.

The fundamental principle for addressing all these challenges is the same: technology serves human creativity and relationship rather than directing it. When challenges arise, the solution is usually more human connection and clearer agreements about how AI assistance supports rather than replaces the relational foundation of meaningful innovation.

IX. Professional Development for the AI-Empowered Facilitator

Facilitating innovation with AI companions requires developing new capabilities that blend traditional facilitation skills with technological literacy and ethical awareness. This isn't just about learning to use new tools—it's about evolving professional identity to thrive in human-AI collaborative relationships.

Narrative Listening involves capturing stories as raw materials for co-creation rather than just information to be organized. AI can help analyze storytelling patterns, identify thematic connections across different narratives, and suggest metaphors that bridge different perspectives.

But the essential skill of recognizing which stories carry emotional weight, cultural significance, or transformative potential remains fundamentally human. Facilitators must develop sensitivity to the stories that want to be told, the wisdom that emerges between words, and the cultural contexts that give narrative meaning.

Tool Temperance means knowing when *not* to use technological assistance, recognizing that some moments require purely human attention. Innovation often happens in subtle relational dynamics—

moments of vulnerability, creative risk, or cultural bridge-building that can be disrupted by technological mediation.

Effective facilitators develop intuition about when AI assistance will enhance collaborative creativity and when it will interrupt the human chemistry that makes breakthrough thinking possible.

Emotional Literacy extends beyond reading individual emotional states to understanding group emotional dynamics and how they interact with technological assistance. Some groups thrive with constant AI input, while others need extended periods of purely human interaction before they can productively engage with technological suggestions.

Ethical Framing involves bringing moral clarity to prompts, outputs, and the overall design of innovation processes. This includes asking whose voices are missing from AI training data, whose perspectives might be marginalized by technological assistance, and how innovation outcomes will affect stakeholders who aren't present in the room.

I advise facilitators to build *rituals* around reflection that help them maintain awareness of their own learning edges, values alignment, and capacity for soulful practice. The AI can suggest reflection prompts, but only humans can interpret those prompts in light of their deepest purposes for facilitating transformative work.

Facilitation in the Intelligence Age isn't mechanical—it's **musical**, requiring sensitivity to rhythm, harmony, and the spaces between notes where meaning often emerges.

X. Looking Forward: Innovation as Sacred Dialogue

Innovation is not a checklist of creative techniques or a sequence of problem-solving steps. It's a conversation—between our past and our imagined future, between different ways of knowing, between human wisdom and artificial intelligence, between individual insight and collective possibility.

This understanding reframes the facilitator's role from process manager to **sacred dialogue steward**—someone who creates conditions where this multi-dimensional conversation can unfold in ways that honor both human dignity and technological capability.

With intelligent companions, we now have tools that can listen across vast information spaces, identify patterns that human attention might miss, and suggest connections that spark new possibilities. But the heart of innovation facilitation remains fundamentally human—our ability to:

Shape emotional space where people feel safe to share half-formed thoughts, challenge established assumptions, and build on each other's ideas without fear of judgment.

Translate ambiguity into possibility by helping groups stay curious about uncertainty rather than rushing toward premature closure, creating space for breakthrough insights that can only emerge through sustained exploration of complexity.

Build trust across difference by helping diverse participants recognize shared values beneath different perspectives, creating bridges between various ways of thinking that honor rather than homogenize cultural diversity.

Co-create meaning between minds and machines by orchestrating conversations where human values guide technological capability toward outcomes that serve flourishing rather than just efficiency.

The future of innovation facilitation lies not in choosing between human and artificial intelligence, but in developing the wisdom to coordinate them in service of purposes larger than either could serve alone.

The essential insight: *An AI can spark ideas—you decide what becomes a breakthrough. An algorithm can suggest themes—you reveal the soul inside them. A system can accelerate thinking—you ensure it serves meaning.*

Let's keep facilitating forward—not just smartly, but soulfully, with both human wisdom and artificial intelligence serving the sacred work of creating futures worth inhabiting.

CHAPTER 6

The Ethical Compass: Navigating Trust and Transparency

I. The Invisible Architecture of Ethics

"The decisions we embed into technology today become the architecture of society tomorrow."

Ethics in technology is no longer a sidebar conversation relegated to philosophy departments or compliance committees. It has become structural, foundational, urgent. Every interface decision, every algorithmic assumption, every data permission prompt represents a choice about what kind of future we're building and what kinds of relationships we're fostering between humans and intelligent systems.

This shift happened gradually, then suddenly. For decades, technology ethics seemed abstract—interesting for academics but peripheral to practitioners focused on functionality and market success. Then we witnessed algorithmic bias affecting hiring decisions, recommendation systems radicalizing users, and AI-generated content spreading misinformation at unprecedented scale. Suddenly, ethical considerations moved from the margins to the center of technological development.

But even this awakening often treats ethics as risk management—how to avoid harm, prevent lawsuits, or maintain public trust. While these concerns matter, they miss the deeper opportunity that ethical technology represents: the chance to encode human values into systems that will shape billions of interactions, decisions, and relationships.

I've come to understand ethics not as constraint but as **creative catalyst**. When we design technology with genuine care for human dignity, cultural diversity, and long-term flourishing, we often discover solutions that are not only more humane but more effective, sustainable, and broadly beneficial than approaches that optimize for narrow metrics.

When intelligent technology begins to co-author decisions, narratives, and relationships—when AI systems influence how we communicate, what we create, and how we understand ourselves—ethics must shift from external oversight to internal guidance. We need frameworks that help us navigate complexity in real time, not just policies that we apply after problems emerge.

This chapter explores ethics not as limitation on technological progress, but as the **moral imagination** that ensures progress serves human flourishing rather than undermining authentic expression or cultural diversity.

II. Trust Is a Design Feature

Many organizations treat trust as an outcome—something that emerges naturally if products work reliably and marketing communications remain honest. But soulful innovation approaches trust as **a design input**, a foundational requirement that shapes every aspect of how intelligent systems are conceived, built, and deployed.

Trust in human-AI relationships involves several interconnected dimensions:

Transparency extends far beyond simple disclosure to create genuine understanding of how systems work, why they make particular suggestions, and what limitations shape their capabilities. Users need to develop mental models of AI behavior that allow them to collaborate effectively rather than consuming outputs blindly.

I've worked with organizations to design what I call "algorithmic empathy"—explanations that help users understand not just what AI systems do but how they "think" about problems. This might involve showing users the key factors that influenced a recommendation, the confidence level the system has in different predictions, or the alternative approaches it considered but rejected.

Accountability means establishing clear pathways for responsibility when things go wrong, when biases emerge, or when system behavior conflicts with human values. Users need to know not just how to report problems but how those reports will be addressed and what changes might result.

Empathy involves technology that recognizes and responds appropriately to human emotional needs, cultural contexts, and individual circumstances. Systems that demonstrate empathy don't just process requests efficiently—they understand that humans bring complex motivations, anxieties, and hopes to every interaction.

Agency ensures that users maintain meaningful control over their technological relationships, with genuine choices about when and how AI assistance occurs. Trust erodes when people feel manipulated or coerced, even by well-intentioned systems that produce beneficial outcomes.

Let me share an example of how these principles transform user experience. I once advised a startup whose platform used AI to curate mental health resources for users experiencing various challenges. Their initial approach focused on algorithmic accuracy—matching users with resources most likely to help based on symptom patterns and demographic data.

While technically sophisticated, this approach felt invasive and impersonal to many users. People reported feeling "analyzed" rather than supported, leading to low engagement despite high-quality content recommendations.

We redesigned the platform around trust-building rather than optimization. Before offering any suggestions, the system now asks users about their current emotional state, their preferences for different types of support, and their comfort level with various approaches. It explains how it uses this information and allows users to modify or override its reasoning at any point.

Most importantly, we embedded a "Why this suggestion?" feature on every recommendation that helps users understand the thinking behind AI advice. This transparency allowed users to evaluate suggestions intelligently rather than accepting them passively.

The result was counterintuitive: by slowing down the recommendation process and increasing user agency, engagement and satisfaction improved dramatically. Users reported feeling more supported and less surveilled. Trust became the foundation for more effective assistance rather than an obstacle to efficiency.

III. The Moment Technology Began Making Choices

There was a time when tools simply responded to human commands. A hammer struck where we aimed it. A calculator computed what we entered. Even early computers executed instructions without interpretation or adaptation.

But somewhere in the evolution toward intelligent systems, technology began making choices on our behalf—initially small ones, then increasingly significant decisions that shape our daily experience and long-term opportunities.

Consider the micro-choices that AI systems now make routinely:

Information curation determines which emails appear first in our inboxes, which news stories reach our attention, which social media posts we see, and which search results we encounter. These algorithmic choices shape our understanding of reality itself.

Communication mediation influences how our messages are interpreted and presented to others—autocorrect changes our words, tone detection flags potential misunderstandings, translation software mediates cross-cultural communication, and sentiment analysis influences how our expressions are received.

Decision support affects major life choices through credit scoring, job application screening, healthcare diagnosis assistance, and relationship matching. AI systems increasingly participate in decisions about education, employment, housing, and healthcare that determine life trajectories.

Behavioral nudging influences our choices through recommendation engines, interface design, and personalization algorithms that shape what options we see, when we see them, and how they're presented.

These micro-choices accumulate into macro-influences that affect individual opportunities and societal patterns. Yet most of these decisions happen invisibly, without explicit consent or conscious awareness from the people they affect.

The ethical challenge isn't that AI systems make choices—human designers and institutions have always embedded values into tools and systems. The challenge is the **scale, speed, and opacity** at which these choices now operate, and the difficulty of understanding or influencing them after they're deployed.

I've seen organizations struggle with this transition from responsive tools to choice-making partners. A financial services company I worked with discovered that their AI-assisted customer service system had been automatically upgrading some customers to premium services based on communication patterns that correlated with high lifetime value. While technically successful—these customers were indeed satisfied with the upgrades—the practice raised serious ethical questions about consent, transparency, and economic fairness.

The solution required rethinking the entire relationship between efficiency and ethics. Instead of optimizing for revenue outcomes, they redesigned the system to optimize for customer agency. Now the AI identifies opportunities for service improvements but always asks explicit permission before making changes, explains the reasoning behind suggestions, and provides clear options for customers to maintain their current arrangements.

As developers, leaders, and users of intelligent systems, we must ask: *Who taught the system to decide? What worldviews shape its logic? Whose interests are prioritized when choices must be made?* The ethical compass demands we know these answers and take responsibility for shaping them with intention rather than leaving them to emerge accidentally from data patterns or engineering convenience.

IV. Bias Isn't a Bug -- It's an Origin Story

Every system reflects its creators, and bias isn't something that gets accidentally introduced during development—it's baked into the **origin story** of how technology gets conceived, designed, and deployed. Understanding this reality is essential for developing ethical approaches that address root causes rather than just surface symptoms.

Bias operates at multiple levels:

Data bias emerges from historical patterns embedded in training datasets that reflect past discrimination, limited representation, or systemic inequalities. If we train AI systems on hiring data from organizations with poor diversity records, those systems will likely perpetuate discriminatory patterns even if that wasn't the intention.

Design bias reflects the perspectives, priorities, and blind spots of development teams who make countless small choices about functionality, interface design, and system behavior. When design teams lack diversity across multiple dimensions—cultural background, economic experience, age, ability, gender identity—their unconscious assumptions become embedded in technological architecture.

Deployment bias occurs when systems designed for specific contexts get applied more broadly without consideration of different user needs, cultural norms, or structural conditions. A system developed for English-speaking users in affluent markets may function poorly or create unintended harm when deployed in different linguistic or economic contexts.

Feedback bias happens when systems learn primarily from users who are most comfortable engaging with technology, whose communication styles match system expectations, or who have time and resources to provide detailed input. This creates feedback loops that optimize for some user experiences while neglecting others.

Rather than treating bias as a technical problem to be solved through better algorithms, intelligent technology with soul approaches bias as a **design challenge** that requires diverse perspectives, cultural sensitivity, and ongoing commitment to equity and inclusion.

I worked with a healthcare AI company that discovered their diagnostic assistance system performed significantly worse for patients whose symptoms didn't match typical presentation patterns found in their training data. Rather than simply adding more diverse data, they fundamentally redesigned their approach to include community health workers and cultural liaisons in the development process.

The result was a system that not only performed better across different populations but also helped healthcare providers recognize their own diagnostic biases and develop more culturally responsive practices. Addressing AI bias became an opportunity to address human bias and systemic healthcare inequities.

Intelligent technology with soul confronts bias not with defensiveness or technical fixes, but with **transparency, accountability, and ongoing recalibration** guided by communities most likely to be affected by algorithmic decisions.

We must treat bias not as shame but as signal—information that helps us understand whose voices need to be included, what perspectives have been overlooked, and how systems can be redesigned to serve broader human flourishing rather than replicating existing inequalities.

V. Designing for Ethical Tension

Real ethics lives in **gray zones** where competing values create genuine dilemmas that don't have simple solutions. Traditional approaches to technology ethics often seek to eliminate this tension through policies, guidelines, and automated decision-making. But soulful systems recognize that ethical tension is often a source of wisdom that should be surfaced and explored rather than hidden or resolved prematurely.

Consider some fundamental tensions that emerge in intelligent technology design:

Privacy vs. Personalization—Users often want systems that understand their preferences, anticipate their needs, and adapt to their communication styles. But this personalization requires collecting and analyzing personal information in ways that might compromise privacy or feel invasive.

Equity vs. Scale—Designing systems that serve diverse populations fairly often requires customization, cultural adaptation, and resource-intensive human oversight that can conflict with the efficiency gains that make technology broadly affordable and accessible.

Speed vs. Empathy—Market pressures and user expectations often favor rapid response and immediate solutions, but meaningful human support frequently requires patience, reflection, and the kind of nuanced understanding that takes time to develop.

Autonomy vs. Oversight—People value freedom to make their own choices and control their own experiences, but they also benefit from guidance, protection, and safeguards that might limit their immediate autonomy in service of long-term well-being.

Rather than resolving these tensions through predetermined trade-offs, soulful systems create space for ongoing negotiation that honors the complexity of human values and circumstances.

I once worked with a healthcare AI team who faced exactly this kind of ethical dilemma: Should their system automatically flag patients for mental health interventions based on predicted risk factors, or should it wait for explicit human oversight before taking any action?

Automatic flagging could save lives by identifying people in crisis who might not seek help independently. But it also raised serious concerns about privacy, consent, and the potential for algorithmic bias to disproportionately target certain communities for unwanted mental health attention.

Instead of choosing between these competing values, we designed a layered approach that honored both safety and autonomy:

- **AI-proposed tiers** where the system identifies potential risk levels and suggests intervention options without automatically implementing them
- **Human teams validated** these assessments with social context, cultural sensitivity, and relationship-based understanding that algorithms cannot provide
- **Feedback loops refined** future predictions based on outcomes and patient experiences, improving both accuracy and cultural responsiveness over time
- **Transparency protocols** ensured that patients understood how risk assessment worked and maintained agency over their participation in the system

The resulting approach wasn't as fast as full automation or as thorough as purely human assessment, but it honored the complexity of mental healthcare in ways that built trust with both patients and providers.

This system became not just accurate but **humble**—acknowledging its limitations while contributing valuable capabilities to human-centered care. It made space for ethical tension rather than resolving it artificially, creating opportunities for wisdom to emerge from the ongoing negotiation between competing values.

VI. Transparency Is an Act of Generosity

Too often, technological systems hide their logic "under the hood" in ways that might protect intellectual property or simplify user interfaces but also create opacity that undermines trust and agency. Soulful transparency isn't just explanation—it's **invitation** to understand, participate, and maintain meaningful control over technological relationships.

Effective transparency allows users to explore several dimensions of system behavior:

Reasoning transparency helps users understand why particular recommendations appeared, what factors influenced specific suggestions, and how different inputs might lead to different outputs. This goes beyond simple "the algorithm did it" explanations to provide genuine insight into logical processes.

Data transparency reveals what information systems use to make decisions, where that information comes from, how it gets processed, and what assumptions guide its interpretation. Users deserve to know what digital footprints shape their technological experiences.

Limitation transparency acknowledges what systems cannot do, where they tend to make mistakes, and what human oversight remains necessary. This prevents both over-reliance on AI assistance and disappointment when systems fail to meet unrealistic expectations.

Values transparency makes explicit the principles and priorities embedded in system design, helping users understand whose interests are served and what trade-offs guide technological behavior.

Control transparency clarifies what aspects of system behavior users can influence, how to exercise that influence, and what changes are possible through feedback or customization.

In my consulting work, I've found that transparency often improves rather than undermines system effectiveness. When users understand how technology works, they become better collaborative partners who can provide more relevant input and use outputs more appropriately.

For example, I worked with an educational technology company whose AI tutoring system was producing excellent learning outcomes but low user satisfaction. Students reported feeling frustrated and confused by the system's teaching approach, even when it was helping them learn effectively.

We implemented what we called "pedagogical transparency"—features that helped students understand why the system was presenting material in particular sequences, what learning objectives guided lesson design, and how their performance data influenced future content recommendations.

We also added "teaching philosophy" explanations that connected AI tutoring strategies to established educational research, helping students understand the human wisdom embedded in algorithmic instruction.

The result was remarkable: learning outcomes improved even further because students became active participants in their educational experience rather than passive recipients of algorithmic instruction. They learned not just subject matter but also how to learn more effectively by understanding the principles behind effective teaching.

This transparency turned the AI tutor from a mysterious black box into a **trusted educational partner** that students could collaborate with more effectively. They began providing better feedback about their learning preferences, taking more ownership of their educational progress, and developing metacognitive skills that served them beyond their interaction with the AI system.

Transparency becomes **generous** when it enables rather than overwhelms, when it increases rather than decreases user agency, and when it builds rather than erodes trust in technological relationships.

VII. The Ethics of Emotional Resonance

Modern intelligent systems increasingly demonstrate emotional capabilities—detecting mood, adapting tone, responding to stress, and calibrating communication style based on emotional cues. While these capabilities can enhance human-AI collaboration, they also raise profound ethical questions about manipulation, authenticity, and the boundaries of appropriate technological intervention in human emotional experience.

The central ethical question isn't whether AI systems should recognize emotions—they already do. The question is **to what end** and **with what constraints** should emotional intelligence be deployed in technological relationships.

Emotional calibration that honors authenticity asks: Does this adaptation help humans express themselves more clearly, or does it pressure them to conform to algorithmic expectations? Does tone-shifting promote genuine communication, or does it erase important emotional information that others need to receive?

I once encountered an AI system that automatically softened assertive language in workplace communications, ostensibly to reduce conflict and improve collaboration. While well-intentioned, this "emotional smoothing" had problematic effects, particularly for women and people from cultures that were already pressured to communicate less directly.

A manager who needed to set clear boundaries with a chronically late employee found that the AI system kept suggesting softer language that diluted her message's clarity and authority. The "improved" communication actually undermined her ability to address the performance issue effectively.

We redesigned the system to ask contextual questions before offering emotional adjustments: "Is this message meant to challenge or comfort?" "Do you want to prioritize directness or diplomacy?" "How important is it that the recipient understand your boundaries clearly?"

These questions helped users make conscious choices about emotional calibration rather than accepting algorithmic assumptions about appropriate communication styles. The system learned to support rather than override human emotional intelligence.

Emotional support that maintains appropriate boundaries recognizes the difference between providing helpful technological assistance and attempting to replace human connection, therapy, or meaningful relationships.

AI systems can remind us to take breaks when stress indicators appear, suggest language that builds rather than damages relationships, and help us recognize emotional patterns that affect our work and relationships. But they cannot and should not attempt to meet deeper human needs for understanding, belonging, and unconditional acceptance that only authentic human relationships can provide.

Emotional consent ensures that people choose when and how their emotional states become part of technological analysis. Just as we wouldn't want humans analyzing our emotions without permission, we need clear protocols for when AI systems can detect, respond to, or act on emotional information.

This might involve explicit emotional sharing ("I'm feeling overwhelmed today and would appreciate gentler communication") rather than algorithmic detection, or clear opt-in processes for emotional monitoring with transparent explanations of how that information gets used.

The goal is emotional technology that **honors rather than manipulates** human feelings, that **supports rather than replaces** emotional intelligence, and that **enhances rather than erodes** our capacity for authentic relationship with ourselves and others.

VIII. Consent as Ongoing Relationship

Traditional technology approaches consent as a checkbox—a one-time agreement that grants broad permission for data collection and system behavior. But soulful technological relationships treat consent as **a living conversation** that evolves as both human needs and system capabilities change over time.

This ongoing consent model recognizes several important realities:

People's comfort levels change as they gain experience with technology, as their life circumstances shift, and as they develop better understanding of how their data gets used and what control they can exercise.

System capabilities evolve in ways that might create new opportunities for beneficial assistance or new risks for privacy and autonomy that weren't anticipated in original consent agreements.

Context matters for consent in ways that blanket permissions cannot address. Someone might be comfortable with AI assistance during work hours but want privacy during personal time, or they might welcome emotional support during stressful periods while preferring independence during stable times.

Relationship depth develops over time, and people might become willing to share more information or accept more assistance as trust builds through positive experiences.

Effective ongoing consent includes several practical elements:

Granular control that allows users to specify different permission levels for different types of assistance, different times of day, or different life contexts. Rather than all-or-nothing choices, people need nuanced options that reflect the complexity of their actual preferences and needs.

Regular check-ins that prompt users to review and update their consent preferences, particularly when system capabilities expand or usage patterns change significantly.

Easy modification that makes changing consent settings as simple as changing other preferences, without penalty or friction that might discourage people from exercising control over their technological relationships.

Clear consequences that help users understand what they gain and lose through different consent choices, without pressure or manipulation that might influence decisions inappropriately.

In one platform redesign I guided, we replaced a traditional privacy policy with what we called "Consent Journaling"—user-facing logs that showed data access over time, explained how information was being used, and provided simple interfaces for modifying sharing preferences.

Users could see patterns in their own data sharing, understand the relationship between information they provided and assistance they received, and make informed decisions about future consent based on actual experience rather than hypothetical scenarios.

The result was increased rather than decreased data sharing because users felt genuinely informed and empowered rather than confused or coerced. Trust increased because people could see evidence that their consent choices were being honored and that they maintained meaningful control over their technological relationships.

Consent becomes **relational** rather than transactional when it honors the dynamic nature of human values, needs, and circumstances while maintaining clear boundaries around respect and agency.

IX. Building Ethical Feedback Loops

Soulful systems must be teachable—capable of learning not just from usage patterns and performance metrics, but from explicit feedback about values alignment, cultural sensitivity, and ethical impact. This requires designing feedback mechanisms that capture the qualitative dimensions of human experience that quantitative analytics often miss.

Three key practices enable ethical learning in AI systems:

Ethical Annotations allow users to flag specific instances where system behavior conflicts with their values, feels culturally insensitive, or produces unintended consequences. These annotations become training data for improving ethical behavior rather than just technical performance.

For example, users might flag when AI-generated content feels stereotypical, when recommendation algorithms seem to reflect bias, or when automation creates barriers for people with disabilities. These flags help systems learn to recognize and avoid patterns that cause harm even when they might optimize traditional metrics.

Responsiveness Protocols define how systems adapt based on ethical feedback, ensuring that user concerns translate into actual improvements in system behavior rather than just data collection without action.

This might involve immediate adjustments to individual user experiences, broader policy changes when patterns of concern emerge, or expanded human oversight when feedback reveals systematic problems that require more than algorithmic solutions.

Reflection Prompts ask users to consider the broader impact of their technological interactions, helping both humans and systems develop better understanding of ethical implications over time.

Rather than just asking "Was this helpful?" feedback systems might prompt questions like "Did this interaction feel respectful of your cultural background?" or "How did this assistance affect your sense of agency and control?" or "What concerns would you want others to know about this technology?"

I've seen these feedback approaches transform AI systems from static rule-followers into dynamic learning partners that develop better ethical judgment through ongoing dialogue with diverse human communities.

In one project, an AI writing assistant learned to recognize when it was homogenizing different cultural communication styles by responding to user feedback about authenticity and cultural appropriateness. Instead of optimizing for generic "clarity," it learned to preserve cultural voice while offering technical improvements.

The system developed sensitivity to contexts where communication differences reflected important cultural values that shouldn't be smoothed away, versus situations where technical assistance could genuinely improve cross cultural understanding without erasing identity.

This ethical learning happened through iterative feedback from users who felt safe flagging concerns and confident that their input would influence system behavior. Feedback became **co-creation** rather than evaluation, transforming both human and artificial intelligence through ongoing ethical dialogue.

X. Ethics in Collaboration: People + Machines

When teams collaborate with intelligent tools, ethics becomes a **shared responsibility** that requires ongoing attention from all participants—human and artificial. This shared ethical stewardship involves several key practices:

Explicit role mapping clarifies what decisions are human-driven versus system-suggested, ensuring that responsibility remains clear even when collaboration becomes fluid and interactive.

Assumption challenging creates regular opportunities for teams to examine the values and biases embedded in their technological partnerships, questioning whether AI assistance is serving their stated intentions or inadvertently undermining other important goals.

Impact consideration expands awareness beyond immediate team productivity to consider how human-AI collaboration affects stakeholders who aren't present in the room—customers, communities, future users, and society more broadly.

Values alignment checking provides structured opportunities to assess whether technological collaboration is supporting or contradicting the deeper purposes and principles that guide team work.

In innovation sessions I facilitate, I make these ethical dimensions explicit rather than leaving them implicit. I might say: "This suggestion came from our AI partner—let's treat it as a thought partner's input rather than expert authority, and consider how it aligns with the values we articulated earlier."

This framing helps teams maintain agency while benefiting from artificial intelligence capabilities. It prevents what I call "algorithmic abdication"—the tendency to defer to AI suggestions without conscious consideration of whether they serve human intentions.

I also build in regular "ethical check-ins" where teams pause to reflect on their collaborative process: "How is our partnership with AI affecting our decision-making?" "Are we maintaining responsibility for the consequences of our choices?" "What voices or perspectives might we be overlooking because we're focused on technological efficiency?"

These check-ins help teams notice when technological convenience might be undermining ethical reflection, when speed might be compromising thoughtfulness, or when AI capabilities might be replacing rather than supporting human judgment.

Ethics thrives when no one human or machine—assumes moral authority or absolution. Distributed ethical responsibility requires ongoing dialogue, mutual accountability, and the humility to recognize that both human and artificial intelligence have limitations that require collaborative wisdom to address effectively.

XI. The Ethical Compass Framework

Through years of working with organizations navigating ethical challenges in AI deployment, I've developed a practical framework that helps teams maintain ethical orientation while making complex decisions in rapidly changing technological contexts.

This **Ethical Compass** provides direction rather than destination, offering principles that guide decision-making rather than rules that determine outcomes:

Transparency asks: What is being done, why is it happening, and how can affected parties understand and influence these processes? This principle prioritizes openness, explanation, and user agency over efficiency or proprietary protection.

Practical applications include layered explanations that help users understand system behavior at appropriate levels of detail, disclosure of data sources and processing methods, and clear pathways for users to influence or opt out of algorithmic decision-making.

Empathy inquires: How does this technology affect people emotionally, culturally, and relationally? This principle ensures that efficiency gains don't come at the expense of human dignity, authentic expression, or cultural identity.

This might involve tone-checking that honors rather than homogenizes communication styles, cultural sensitivity review that ensures technology serves diverse communities appropriately, and emotional impact assessment that considers psychological as well as functional effects.

Accountability demands: Who takes responsibility for decisions, and how are problems addressed when they arise? This principle establishes clear pathways for oversight, feedback, and improvement that maintain human agency over technological systems.

Practical elements include feedback systems that clarify human and machine responsibilities, escalation protocols that ensure serious concerns reach appropriate decision-makers, and learning processes that translate ethical feedback into system improvements.

Flexibility questions: Can the system evolve with changing values, circumstances, and understanding? This principle recognizes that ethical technology must be adaptive rather than rigid, capable of learning and improving rather than locked into initial design assumptions.

This includes feedback loops that capture user concerns and suggestions, regular review processes that assess ethical impact over time, and update mechanisms that allow systems to incorporate new ethical insights and changing community values.

Purpose Alignment confirms: Does this technology reflect what matters most to the people and communities it serves? This principle ensures that technological capability serves human values rather than replacing them with algorithmic optimization.

Applications include values checkpoints that connect daily decisions to larger purposes, stakeholder engagement processes that include affected communities in system design, and impact assessment that considers long-term as well as immediate consequences.

This compass helps teams reframe ethics not as constraint but as **clarity**—guidance that actually improves decision-making by ensuring that technological choices serve authentic human needs and values.

Rather than slowing down innovation, ethical compass navigation often accelerates meaningful progress by preventing costly mistakes, building stronger stakeholder relationships, and creating sustainable solutions that serve broader constituencies over longer time horizons.

XII. Looking Forward: Ethics as Invitation

Technology is now part of every significant conversation, decision, and relationship in professional and personal life. Its voice matters. Its choices ripple through communities, economies, and cultures in ways we're only beginning to understand.

As we build, deploy, and relate to intelligent systems, ethics must be at the table not just as compliance or risk management, but as

character—the moral imagination that shapes what we choose to create and how we choose to create it.

The future of human-AI collaboration will be determined not by technological capability alone, but by the wisdom, courage, and care we bring to designing relationships that honor both human dignity and artificial intelligence potential.

This requires moving beyond reactive ethics that responds to problems after they emerge toward **proactive ethics** that anticipates challenges and designs solutions that prevent harm while enabling beneficial outcomes.

It means including diverse voices in technological development, not as afterthoughts but as essential collaborators whose perspectives shape fundamental design decisions.

It requires transparency that enables genuine understanding and agency rather than performative disclosure that creates appearance of openness without substance.

Most importantly, it demands that we treat ethical consideration not as obstacle to innovation but as **creative catalyst** that often leads to more effective, sustainable, and broadly beneficial solutions than approaches that optimize for narrow technical or economic criteria.

Trust isn't claimed—it's cultivated through countless small choices that demonstrate genuine care for human flourishing. Transparency isn't optional—it's the foundation of collaborative relationships that honor both human agency and artificial capability. Ethics isn't limitation—it's leadership that ensures technological progress serves the deepest human values and highest aspirations.

Let's continue building the future with both intelligence and integrity, ensuring that the systems we create reflect the wisdom and care we want to see in the world.

PART III

Expression, Story, and Systems

CHAPTER 7

Crafting Narrative: AI Meets Storytelling

I. Story Is Structure

"Narrative isn't decoration --- it's architecture. It holds the meaning that facts alone cannot carry."

From my earliest days in an Italian-American household, story was everywhere—woven into daily existence like the aroma of garlic and basil that perpetually filled our kitchen. Stories were told at dinner tables where three generations gathered each Sunday, folded into bedtime rituals that connected us to ancestors we'd never met, carried across decades like precious heirlooms that gained meaning with each retelling.

My grandmother didn't simply recount events—she architected experience. When she described her journey from Sicily to Ellis Island, every detail served a larger narrative purpose. The rough wool of her only coat became a symbol of resilience. The strange sounds of English in her ears transformed into metaphor for courage in the face of uncertainty. The first American dollar she earned wasn't just currency—it was tangible proof that dreams could survive translation across oceans and languages.

These weren't just family chronicles. They were masterclasses in narrative construction. Through these stories, I learned that narrative isn't a tool—it's a way of knowing, a fundamental human technology for transforming raw experience into wisdom, isolated events into coherent meaning, individual struggle into universal truth.

Professionally, I've built strategy around story for three decades. In corporate boardrooms, I've watched executives flounder with spreadsheets and data visualizations until someone shared the narrative that gave numbers their soul. In classrooms, I've seen students come alive not when presented with theoretical frameworks, but when invited into stories that made abstract concepts personally relevant and emotionally resonant.

In innovation sessions, I've observed teams generate brilliant technical solutions that died in implementation until they discovered the story that connected their work to larger human purposes. The most successful organizational transformations I've facilitated began not with process redesign or system upgrades, but with narrative reconstruction—helping people understand their current challenges and future possibilities as chapters in a larger story worth telling.

Now, intelligent technology meets us at this narrative frontier. AI systems can mirror tone with remarkable sophistication, suggest story arcs that follow classical dramatic structures, reorder plot elements for maximum emotional impact, and even generate entire narratives that feel authentically human. But crafting narrative soulfully requires more than technical functionality—it demands intention, cultural sensitivity, and deep understanding of how stories create meaning rather than merely convey information.

This chapter explores how storytelling and intelligent systems can co-create meaning that honors both human wisdom and artificial capability, while keeping the human heartbeat—the rhythm of authentic experience and inherited cultural memory—at the center of every narrative we craft together.

II. Why Narrative Matters More Than Ever

In our current moment of information overload and attention fragmentation, narrative becomes more than communication strategy—it becomes survival technology. Story is how we filter overwhelming complexity into manageable understanding, how we connect emotionally across difference and distance, how we build coherence from chaos, and how we shape identity in digital ecosystems that can feel alienating and depersonalizing.

The sheer volume of information available daily would have been incomprehensible to previous generations. We encounter more data in a single day than many of our ancestors processed in entire lifetimes. Yet information without narrative context often creates anxiety rather than understanding, noise rather than insight, confusion rather than clarity.

When professionals clarify their narrative—when they understand not just what they do but why it matters and how it connects to larger human purposes—they move from reactive response to intentional action. I've coached leaders who were drowning in metrics and market analysis until they discovered the story that reframed their decisions from tactical responses to strategic choices aligned with deeper values.

Consider the difference between a data presentation showing declining customer retention rates and a narrative that explains those numbers as symptoms of a relationship crisis—a breakdown in the story customers tell themselves about why they chose to engage with your organization. The first approach leads to tactical fixes: better pricing, enhanced features, improved customer service protocols. The narrative approach reveals the need for fundamental relationship reconstruction: understanding what story you want to tell together and how your organization can play a more meaningful role in customers' own life narratives.

I've worked with organizations that achieved remarkable turnarounds not by changing their products or services, but by changing their story—both the story they told about themselves and the story they invited others to participate in. When people understand their work as contributing to narratives larger than immediate tasks or quarterly objectives, engagement deepens, innovation accelerates, and resilience strengthens.

AI tools now support storytelling in unprecedented ways, but they cannot replace the fundamentally human work of meaning-making. They are sophisticated scaffolds that can help us organize narrative elements, refine emotional pacing, and explore alternative story structures. But they cannot provide the cultural wisdom, emotional intelligence, and values clarity that give stories their power to transform understanding and inspire action.

The relationship between human storytelling and artificial intelligence is collaborative—each bringing distinctive capabilities to the ancient human practice of making meaning through narrative.

III. The Narrative Intelligence of AI

Artificial intelligence systems now demonstrate remarkable capabilities in understanding, generating, and manipulating narrative elements. Understanding both what these systems can offer storytellers and their limitations is crucial for authentic human-AI narrative collaboration.

Structural Support represents AI's most reliable contribution to narrative craft. These systems excel at organizing paragraphs for logical flow, calibrating emotional pacing across long documents, sequencing arguments for maximum persuasive impact, and identifying structural patterns that strengthen narrative coherence.

I've worked with AI systems that can recognize when a story lacks adequate setup for its climax, when emotional intensity needs modulation to prevent reader fatigue, or when transitions between sections feel abrupt rather than organic. These structural insights often help writers see their own work more clearly, identifying problems they felt intuitively but couldn't articulate precisely.

Language Calibration involves AI's capacity to adjust formality levels, accessibility, and rhythm to match different audiences and purposes. The same core narrative might need to be told with academic precision for scholarly publication, conversational warmth for popular media, or inspirational energy for organizational communications.

Rather than requiring authors to manually translate their stories across different registers, AI can suggest language modifications that preserve essential meaning while adapting tone and style to serve different communicative contexts. This capability is particularly valuable for complex narratives that need to reach diverse audiences without losing their essential character.

Context Echo describes AI's ability to link current narrative elements back to earlier metaphors, themes, or character developments, reinforcing narrative anchors that create coherence across extended works. Human authors sometimes lose track of subtle patterns they've established, especially in long-form writing where maintaining consistency becomes challenging.

AI systems can track thematic threads, character voice patterns, and metaphorical frameworks across entire manuscripts, suggesting moments where callback references might strengthen overall narrative unity or where inconsistencies might confuse readers.

Emotional Cueing involves AI's growing capacity to suggest moments for pause, emphasis, tension, or release based on analysis of emotional flow patterns that engage readers most effectively. These systems can identify when narrative pacing feels rushed or when emotional intensity needs variation to maintain reader engagement.

More sophisticated AI can suggest when personal vulnerability might deepen reader connection, when abstract concepts need grounding in concrete story, or when intellectual complexity needs emotional counterbalance to remain accessible.

In my own manuscript development work, I've experienced these capabilities firsthand. While working on a chapter about organizational culture change, an AI partner suggested reframing "Innovation with AI Companions" as "Co-Creating Futures with Intelligent Partners." The revised phrase felt more storied—it suggested narrative possibility rather than technical process, collaborative adventure rather than tool usage.

This wasn't simple word substitution or optimization. The AI had engaged with the emotional undertone I was seeking, understood the relational emphasis that mattered to my audience, and offered language that better served my narrative intention. That's not automation—that's **alignment through contextual understanding**.

IV. Storytelling with AI: A Partnership Model

Through extensive experience collaborating with AI systems across various storytelling contexts, I've developed a **narrative partnership**

model that maximizes the creative potential of human-AI collaboration while preserving the essentially human elements that give stories their soul.

This partnership approach treats AI not as a ghostwriter or content generator, but as a **narrative partner**—a sophisticated collaborator that brings complementary capabilities to the storytelling process while respecting human authorship and cultural wisdom.

My typical workflow involves five distinct phases that leverage both human and artificial intelligence:

Story Prompting begins each project by sharing origin anecdotes, cultural contexts, and emotional anchors that provide the AI with rich background for understanding the deeper purposes behind the narrative. Rather than simply describing plot points or content objectives, I share the personal experiences, family stories, or cultural memories that gave birth to the story I want to tell.

During this phase, AI systems often ask clarifying questions that help me articulate assumptions I didn't realize I was making: "What does success mean to the communities you're writing for?" "How does this story connect to your own cultural inheritance?" "What transformation are you hoping to facilitate through this narrative?"

These questions serve as creative catalysts that help me discover layers of meaning and purpose that might otherwise remain implicit or underdeveloped.

Structural Mapping involves collaborative development of narrative arcs that serve both classical storytelling principles and the specific communicative goals of each project. We work together to identify the essential movements of the story: challenge → tension → insight → transformation, but with attention to cultural storytelling patterns that might diverge from European narrative traditions.

AI can suggest multiple structural approaches—linear progression, circular storytelling, episodic development, or thematic organization—while I provide cultural and emotional criteria for choosing among these options. The goal is finding structures that feel authentic to the story being told rather than imposing predetermined frameworks.

Tone Calibration requires ongoing dialogue about rhythm, emotional intensity, and voice consistency. AI systems can suggest places where pacing might be adjusted to prevent reader fatigue, where emotional peaks and valleys might be rebalanced, or where voice consistency might be strengthened.

But I maintain responsibility for cultural authenticity and emotional truth. When an AI suggests smoother transitions, I consider whether that smoothness serves clarity or eliminates meaningful roughness that reflects authentic cultural voice or emotional complexity.

Metaphor Layering involves AI's capacity to propose imagery and symbolic frameworks based on semantic analysis of existing content, while I evaluate these suggestions against cultural appropriateness, emotional resonance, and thematic coherence.

AI might notice that I've been using organic metaphors—growth, roots, flowering—and suggest extensions of that metaphorical framework. But I decide whether those extensions honor the cultural traditions that gave birth to my metaphorical thinking or whether they feel artificially imposed.

Emotional Mirror provides opportunities for collaborative review of narrative flow, with AI highlighting potential reader fatigue points, emotional overwhelm, or pacing that might feel rushed or dragged. These technical observations serve human decisions about how to balance authenticity with accessibility, depth with engagement.

In one memorable collaboration, I was describing a facilitation session as "noisy and chaotic." The AI paused our work and asked: "Would 'symphonic' capture both the chaos and the underlying beauty you're describing?"

The suggestion was revelatory. "Symphonic" suggested intentional complexity rather than mere confusion, collaborative music rather than random noise. It honored both the challenging aspects of group creativity and the ultimate harmony that emerged from apparent discord. The resulting revision sang with energy that the original description had missed.

This exchange illustrated what narrative partnership can achieve: human cultural wisdom and emotional intelligence meeting artificial pattern recognition and linguistic facility to create expression that neither could achieve independently.

V. Preserving Cultural Narrative in a Digital World

Story lives in culture, carrying forward the wisdom, rhythms, and meaning-making patterns of communities across generations. Intelligent systems, trained primarily on dominant cultural patterns and mainstream literary traditions, risk flattening this heritage into homogenized "effective communication" that loses the very distinctiveness that gives different cultural narratives their power.

As someone deeply connected to Italian-American storytelling traditions, I work deliberately to protect cultural elements that might seem "inefficient" to AI systems optimized for clarity and accessibility:

Idiomatic rhythm includes the natural speech patterns, pauses, and emphasis structures that reflect how stories are told within specific cultural communities. Italian-American narrative often involves circular storytelling, where the point emerges gradually through layered repetition and emotional buildup rather than direct linear progression.

AI systems frequently suggest "improvements" that would eliminate this circularity in favor of more direct communication. But those circular patterns aren't inefficiency—they're cultural technology for building emotional connection and ensuring that wisdom gets transmitted alongside information.

Non-linear structures reflect different cultural approaches to organizing meaning and time. Some storytelling traditions prioritize relationship and emotional truth over chronological accuracy, weaving past and present together in ways that honor the interconnectedness of experience across generations.

When AI suggests reorganizing these non-linear narratives into more logical sequences, I often decline because the apparent confusion serves deeper cultural purposes—helping readers experience the way memory actually works, the way family wisdom gets transmitted, the way meaningful events exist outside simple chronology.

Emotional pauses and evocative phrasing create space for readers to feel as well as think, to connect personally with universal themes. These elements might slow down information processing but speed up emotional engagement and cultural recognition.

Food, faith, and family motifs carry specific cultural meanings that resist translation into generic symbols. When I write about Sunday dinners, I'm not just describing meals—I'm invoking entire systems of relationship, obligation, celebration, and cultural transmission that shaped my understanding of how humans care for each other.

AI systems sometimes suggest replacing these specific cultural references with more universal symbols that might reach broader audiences. But that universalization often drains the narrative of precisely the cultural specificity that gives it authenticity and emotional power.

In one particularly revealing collaboration, I used a layered sentence structure that cascaded like my grandmother's way of building to important points: "And so we learned—not through instruction but through example, not through rules but through rhythm, not through words but through the way she moved through her kitchen like a woman who understood that feeding people was a form of prayer—that love gets expressed through attention to detail."

The AI offered a streamlined revision: "We learned through her example that cooking was her way of expressing love."

While more efficient, the revision eliminated the cultural rhythm that made the original sentence feel authentic to my family's storytelling tradition. I declined the suggestion because some stories require resistance to reduction, because the way something is said often carries as much meaning as what is being said.

To preserve cultural nuance in digital storytelling collaborations, I've developed several practical strategies:

- **Annotating AI corrections with cultural intent**—explaining why apparent inefficiencies serve important cultural purposes
- **Curating training phrases that reflect heritage patterns**—providing AI with examples of authentic cultural voice to improve future suggestions
- **Building personal glossaries of cultural symbolism**—helping AI understand the specific meanings that particular images, phrases, or references carry within my cultural context

- **Setting boundaries around cultural sacred spaces**—identifying narrative elements that should remain untouched regardless of technical improvements AI might suggest

Technology can support cultural nuance when we lead it deliberately toward understanding rather than efficiency, when we prioritize authenticity over optimization, and when we remember that the goal of storytelling is not perfect communication but meaningful connection across difference.

VI. Story as Strategic Leadership

Narrative isn't merely personal expression—it's organizational infrastructure that shapes how communities understand their challenges, opportunities, and possibilities. Leaders who master story craft can transform not just communication effectiveness but the fundamental culture and capacity of the groups they serve.

Defining brand through origin myth involves helping organizations articulate not just what they do but why they exist, connecting current activities to founding purposes and cultural values that transcend market positioning. This isn't marketing storytelling—it's identity clarification that guides decision-making when pressures mount and compromise becomes tempting.

One nonprofit I worked with had lost energy and focus after years of adapting to changing funding requirements. Their programs were effective but felt disconnected from each other and from any larger vision. Through narrative work, we rediscovered their founding story: a group of community members who realized that existing social services were treating symptoms rather than addressing root causes of economic insecurity.

That origin story became organizational compass, helping them evaluate new opportunities against the question: "Does this help us address root causes or just manage symptoms?" Their programs gained coherence, their fundraising became more compelling, and their staff rediscovered sense of mission that sustained them through challenging periods.

Navigating crisis with story reframing helps organizations understand disruption not as evidence of failure but as narrative transition that opens new possibilities. Crisis often creates meaning-making crisis—people lose confidence in the stories they've been telling about progress, success, and purpose.

Effective crisis leadership involves helping communities develop new narratives that honor legitimate loss while creating space for adaptation and growth. This requires emotional sophistication that pure problem-solving approaches often miss.

Inspiring teams through collective narrative arcs transforms individual job performance into collaborative contribution to meaningful shared purposes. When people understand their daily work as advancing larger stories they care about, engagement deepens and resilience strengthens.

Rather than managing through metrics and objectives, narrative leaders help teams understand how their current challenges connect to organizational mission, how their individual contributions matter to collective success, and how their shared work participates in larger social and cultural purposes.

AI systems can support these leadership applications in several ways:

Synthesizing stakeholder language to identify shared values and concerns that might not be immediately apparent through traditional communication channels. AI can analyze meeting transcripts, survey responses, and informal communications to surface themes that connect different constituency groups.

Recasting strategy as movement rather than mission by suggesting language that emphasizes dynamic progress toward shared vision rather than static institutional maintenance. This reframing often energizes implementation by connecting current work to larger trajectories of positive change.

Generating metaphors that connect diverse roles within complex organizations, helping different functional areas understand how their work contributes to shared narrative rather than competing for resources or recognition.

In one memorable example, a technology company was struggling with coordination between their engineering, sales, and customer success teams. Each group felt that the others didn't understand or appreciate their contributions to company success.

Working with AI narrative analysis, we discovered that each team was using different metaphors to describe their work: engineers talked about "building elegant solutions," sales people described "connecting with customer needs," and customer success focused on "nurturing long-term relationships."

Rather than trying to homogenize these different perspectives, we developed a unifying narrative that honored all three approaches: the company was "creating technological gardens where elegant design, authentic connection, and patient cultivation combine to help customers flourish."

This metaphorical framework helped each team understand how their distinctive approaches served shared purposes while maintaining their professional identity and expertise.

When leaders speak through story that connects individual effort to collective meaning, organizational culture responds with greater coherence, commitment, and creative capacity to address complex challenges.

VII. Creating Soulful Narrative Artifacts

Soulful stories live beyond the moment of their telling, creating artifacts that preserve not just information but wisdom, relationship dynamics, and cultural insights that can guide future decision-making and relationship building.

Traditional documentation often captures what happened but misses why it mattered, how it felt, and what deeper patterns it revealed about human nature, organizational dynamics, or cultural evolution. Soulful narrative artifacts preserve the full dimensionality of experience in ways that support both practical application and ongoing learning.

Narrative Maps provide visual representations of story flow that combine logical sequence with emotional terrain, helping readers understand not just what happened but how different participants experienced the journey and what meaning emerged through the process.

These maps might track character development through organizational change, showing how different stakeholders moved through resistance, engagement, and ownership as new approaches were implemented. They preserve the human dimension of transformation that traditional project documentation often overlooks.

Voice Guides define tonal markers, metaphorical frameworks, and cultural references that maintain consistency across different platforms and communicators while honoring the cultural specificity that gives organizational narrative its authenticity.

Rather than generic style guides that focus on grammar and formatting, voice guides help future communicators understand the cultural values, emotional ranges, and relational approaches that shape how an organization wants to sound when it speaks to different audiences.

Legacy Statements use AI assistance to support reflective writing that connects current experiences to inherited wisdom and future aspirations. These statements help individuals and organizations understand their work as part of larger historical trajectories that extend beyond immediate objectives.

Legacy statements might explore questions like: "What are we learning that our predecessors didn't have opportunities to understand?" "How does our current work honor the sacrifices that made it possible?" "What do we hope future generations will say about the choices we're making now?"

Emotional Journeys track tone, intensity, and psychological movement through narrative development, providing analysis that helps storytellers understand the emotional experience they're creating for readers while maintaining awareness of cultural storytelling patterns that shouldn't be homogenized for generic effectiveness.

In my own manuscript development work, I've used AI to highlight what I call "emotional terrain"—mapping where warmth increases, where tension spikes, where momentum flags, and where readers might need different types of support or challenge.

This analysis transforms revision from purely technical editing to **soulful cartography**—understanding the landscape of experience I'm creating and making conscious choices about how to guide readers through that landscape in ways that serve both clarity and transformation.

One particularly revealing analysis showed that my writing consistently "warmed up" when I included family stories or cultural references, but "cooled down" when I focused on technical frameworks or abstract concepts. This pattern helped me understand that my most effective teaching happened when I grounded theoretical insights in personal narrative and cultural wisdom.

Rather than simply avoiding technical content, I learned to use family stories and cultural metaphors as bridges that helped readers connect emotionally with abstract concepts, creating narrative architecture that served both intellectual understanding and emotional engagement.

These artifacts help storytellers see not just what they wrote but what they meant—the deeper intentions and cultural patterns that shaped their narrative choices. They create accountability for authenticity while supporting craft development that honors rather than erases cultural distinctiveness.

VIII. The Ethics of Storytelling with AI

Narrative holds tremendous power to shape understanding, influence decisions, and affect relationships across communities and cultures. When intelligent tools begin participating in story creation, we must address ethical considerations that ensure this collaboration serves human dignity rather than undermining authentic expression or cultural diversity.

Consent and representation emerge as primary concerns when AI systems help craft stories that involve other people's experiences, cultural traditions, or community wisdom. Whose stories are we telling, and with what permission? How do we ensure that AI assistance doesn't inadvertently appropriate or misrepresent cultural narratives that don't belong to us?

These questions become particularly complex when AI systems are trained on vast datasets that include cultural expressions from communities that never consented to their stories being used as training material for commercial systems.

I coach authors to embed explicit consent considerations into their AI-assisted storytelling process: "Does this AI suggestion honor my responsibility to the people whose experiences I'm sharing?" "Would this approach feel respectful to the cultural communities whose wisdom I'm drawing from?"

Cultural voice distortion represents another significant concern. AI systems trained primarily on dominant cultural patterns might suggest "improvements" that make stories more accessible to mainstream audiences while erasing the very cultural distinctiveness that gives those stories their authenticity and power.

When AI suggests that my Italian-American circular storytelling should be "streamlined" for efficiency, I must decide whether accessibility serves or undermines my deeper purpose of preserving cultural narrative traditions that risk being lost in digital homogenization.

Emotional surveillance concerns arise when AI systems detect, analyze, and respond to emotional patterns in ways that might feel supportive to some users but invasive to others. The capacity to read emotional undertones in writing can enhance storytelling support, but it can also create uncomfortable experiences of being "analyzed" during vulnerable creative processes.

I recommend building explicit consent protocols around emotional analysis: "Would you like feedback on emotional pacing?" "Are you comfortable with suggestions based on sentiment analysis?" These choices help maintain user agency while allowing those who benefit from emotional support to access it voluntarily.

Authenticity versus optimization creates ongoing tension between AI's capacity to improve technical craft and human responsibility to preserve emotional truth and cultural authenticity. AI might suggest changes that improve readability, engagement, or persuasive impact while eliminating rough edges that reflect authentic emotional experience or cultural voice patterns.

Soulful storytelling with AI requires constant discernment about which suggestions serve authentic expression and which represent algorithmic preferences that might homogenize human experience in problematic ways.

I teach authors to embed regular check-ins throughout their AI collaboration: "Does this suggestion honor my authentic voice and cultural background?" "Would this change improve communication without compromising emotional truth?" "What would my cultural elders think about this modification?"

These questions help maintain accountability to deeper purposes that extend beyond technical craft improvement to encompass cultural stewardship and emotional integrity.

The goal isn't to avoid AI assistance but to use it consciously, ensuring that technological capability serves rather than replaces human wisdom about meaning, culture, and authentic expression.

IX. Legacy Crafting: Story as Inheritance

The deepest stories are those we pass down—narratives that preserve not just family history or organizational memory, but wisdom about how to live with dignity, how to maintain hope during difficulty, and how to contribute meaningfully to communities and causes larger than individual success.

Legacy crafting involves using story to bridge generations, cultures, and contexts, creating inheritance that extends beyond material assets to include moral imagination, cultural wisdom, and practical knowledge about navigating life's fundamental challenges.

AI can support legacy work in several powerful ways:

Collaborative family journals that help multiple generations contribute to shared narrative documents, with AI assistance in organizing different voices, maintaining thematic coherence, and bridging different communication styles across age groups and cultural backgrounds.

These projects often reveal patterns of resilience, adaptation, and wisdom that might otherwise remain invisible to individual family members who experience only portions of larger family stories.

Heritage timeline development that combines AI's organizational capabilities with human cultural knowledge to create comprehensive narratives that connect personal family history to larger historical, cultural, and social contexts.

Rather than simple chronologies, these timelines explore how family decisions intersected with broader social movements, economic changes, and cultural shifts that shaped opportunities and challenges across generations.

Cross-cultural translation that helps preserve stories across language barriers, cultural contexts, and communication preferences while maintaining authenticity and emotional resonance that makes heritage narratives meaningful to contemporary audiences.

This work is particularly important for immigrant families whose stories span multiple languages, cultures, and national contexts, requiring sensitive translation that preserves cultural nuance while making stories accessible to family members who might not share fluency in ancestral languages.

In one deeply moving collaboration, I worked with AI to help craft a tribute to my grandfather that wove together his work ethic, humor, and quiet faith into a unified narrative that captured his character without sentimentalizing his struggles or oversimplifying his complexity.

The AI suggested multiple structural approaches for organizing memories that spanned nearly seven decades of life through dramatic social and economic changes. But the breakthrough came when it helped me recognize a recurring pattern in family stories: my grandfather's consistent approach of meeting challenges through practical action guided by underlying values rather than abstract principles.

This insight led to organizing the tribute around specific examples of how he embodied his values through daily choices—how he treated coworkers during economic depression, how he maintained dignity during discrimination, how he adapted to technological changes without abandoning traditional craftsmanship values.

The AI helped refine language and suggest transitions that strengthened narrative flow, but the emotional core came from family memory and cultural understanding that no algorithm could generate. The collaboration resulted in a tribute that family members still reference years later when making difficult decisions: "What would Grandpa do in this situation?"

The most powerful moment in this collaboration occurred when the AI suggested closing the tribute with: "He didn't tell me how to live—he showed me."

That line captured something essential that had been implicit throughout the narrative but hadn't been directly stated. It reflected a teaching approach that shaped my own understanding of leadership, mentorship, and cultural transmission. The suggestion felt like recognition rather than creation—the AI had recognized a pattern in the story that revealed its deeper meaning.

Legacy narratives become inheritance when they successfully transmit not just information about what happened, but wisdom about how to carry forward values, approaches, and cultural insights that transcend specific historical circumstances.

X. Looking Forward: The Future of Human-AI Narrative Collaboration

As AI systems become more sophisticated in their understanding of language, culture, and emotional nuance, the possibilities for creative collaboration will continue expanding. But the fundamental questions about purpose, authenticity, and cultural stewardship will only become more important.

The trajectory toward deeper partnership suggests that AI systems will develop better understanding of cultural storytelling traditions, more sensitivity to emotional and relational contexts that shape narrative meaning, and greater capacity to support rather than homogenize diverse approaches to story construction.

But this evolution requires human guidance that ensures technological advancement serves cultural diversity rather than erasing it, that supports authentic expression rather than optimizing for algorithmic preferences, and that honors the relational dimensions of storytelling that create community and preserve wisdom across generations.

Emerging challenges include maintaining cultural authenticity in globally connected storytelling environments, preserving space for narrative traditions that resist digital optimization, ensuring that AI assistance doesn't create economic barriers that limit storytelling access to those who can afford sophisticated technological tools, and protecting against algorithmic bias that might favor dominant cultural patterns while marginalizing alternative narrative traditions.

Creative opportunities involve using AI to help preserve endangered storytelling traditions through documentation and translation, supporting cross-cultural narrative collaboration that builds understanding across difference, enabling new forms of interactive storytelling that combine human wisdom with artificial intelligence capabilities, and developing educational approaches that help future storytellers use AI assistance while maintaining cultural authenticity and emotional truth.

The future of narrative in the intelligence age will be shaped by our collective choices about how to integrate technological capability with human wisdom, how to preserve cultural diversity while enabling creative innovation, and how to ensure that the ancient human practice of storytelling continues serving its essential functions of meaning-making, relationship building, and wisdom transmission.

The essential question isn't whether AI can generate compelling narratives—it increasingly can. The question is whether we can develop AI partnership approaches that enhance rather than replace the human elements that make stories transformative: cultural wisdom, emotional authenticity, moral imagination, and the capacity to create meaning that serves human flourishing across generations and communities.

The stories we tell with AI companions today will shape the narrative landscape that future generations inherit. Our responsibility is ensuring that this inheritance includes not just technological capability but also the cultural wisdom, emotional intelligence, and ethical commitment that transform information into wisdom and individual expression into community connection.

Machines can format story—only humans can feel it. Technology can suggest structure—only culture can provide soul. AI can accelerate creation—only wisdom can ensure meaning.

Together, we craft the future of storytelling, line by line, word by word, with both intelligence and soul guiding every choice we make about how stories serve human understanding and community connection.

CHAPTER 8
Futureproofing the Professional

I. More Than Resilience

"The future doesn't just reward skill --- it responds to soul."

Much has been written about future-proofing in the professional realm: upskilling for technological change, adapting to remote work environments, automating routine tasks, and building resilience against economic uncertainty. Corporate training programs promise to teach "21st-century skills." Business schools redesign curricula around "digital transformation." Career coaches advocate for "personal branding" and "continuous learning."

Yet these conversations, however well-intentioned, often miss the deeper dimension that will determine professional relevance in an age of artificial intelligence. They focus on external adaptation—learning new software, mastering new platforms, acquiring new credentials—while overlooking the **inner scaffolding** that prepares professionals not just to survive change, but to steward it with meaning, wisdom, and authentic contribution.

The word "futureproof" itself reveals problematic thinking. It suggests that change is something to defend against rather than partner with, that the future is a threat requiring armor rather than an invitation requiring preparation of heart and mind. It implies that professional value lies in becoming invulnerable to obsolescence rather than becoming increasingly valuable through depth, wisdom, and the capacity to create meaning in whatever circumstances emerge.

True professional preparedness for an intelligent future requires moving beyond transactional skill acquisition to embrace **transformational identity development**. We must equip individuals to partner soulfully with intelligent systems—not just to work with AI, but to lead with it, question it, and co-create alongside it in ways that serve human flourishing rather than mere efficiency.

I've worked with executives who mastered every productivity app and automation tool available, yet found themselves increasingly irrelevant as their organizations sought leaders who could navigate the human dimensions of technological change. I've counseled professionals who accumulated impressive technical credentials but struggled to articulate why their work mattered or how it served purposes larger than their immediate job descriptions.

The future belongs to professionals who understand that technological fluency is table stakes, not competitive advantage. What creates lasting value is the capacity to bring human wisdom, cultural intelligence, emotional depth, and moral imagination to challenges that become more rather than less complex as artificial intelligence automates routine cognitive work.

This chapter offers a roadmap for becoming the kind of professional the future needs most: someone who is aware of technological possibility without being seduced by it, adaptive to change without losing rootedness in values, and aligned with emerging opportunities while remaining anchored in timeless principles about what makes work meaningful and communities thrive.

II. The Shifting Terrain of Professional Identity

The traditional boundaries that once defined professional identity—industry categories, job titles, functional specializations, career trajectories—are becoming increasingly fluid as technological change accelerates and global connectivity reshapes how value gets created and delivered.

Consider what's happening across virtually every sector:

The marketer has become a data scientist, analyzing customer behavior patterns, optimizing algorithmic ad placements, and using AI to personalize content at scale. But they must also remain storytellers who understand human psychology, cultural anthropologists who navigate diverse communities, and relationship builders who create authentic connections in digital environments.

The educator now curates hybrid learning ecosystems that blend human instruction with intelligent tutoring systems, virtual reality experiences, and AI-powered personalization. Yet the essential work remains fundamentally relational: inspiring curiosity, fostering critical thinking, and helping learners develop wisdom alongside knowledge.

The technologist writes code and architects systems, but increasingly becomes a storyteller who helps non-technical stakeholders understand possibilities and trade-offs, an ethicist who considers societal implications of technological choices, and a facilitator who bridges between human needs and machine capabilities.

The strategist partners with algorithms that process vast datasets and model complex scenarios, but must provide the human judgment that determines which questions deserve asking, what outcomes serve human flourishing, and how to maintain organizational values while adapting to changing circumstances.

These shifts demand more than technical retraining. They require **identity evolution** that integrates traditional professional expertise with new capacities for collaboration across human-AI teams, communication across cultural and technological divides, and leadership through uncertainty that no amount of data analysis can fully resolve.

Professional identity in the intelligence age becomes less about functional specialization and more about **integrative capacity**—the ability to bridge between different domains of knowledge, different types of intelligence, and different communities of practice in service of challenges that no single expertise can address adequately.

III. Beyond Skillsets: Cultivating Mindsets

The professional development industry has become obsessed with skillsets—specific technical competencies that can be taught in workshops, measured through assessments, and added to résumés like merit badges. While technical skills remain important, they represent only the surface layer of professional capacity.

The deeper work involves cultivating **mindsets**—ways of thinking, being, and relating that determine how technical skills get applied and whether they serve meaningful purposes. Mindsets shape what problems we notice, what solutions we consider, what values guide our decisions, and how we collaborate with others in pursuit of shared goals.

Futureproof professionals must develop qualities that artificial intelligence cannot replicate:

Discernment represents the capacity to make sense of ambiguity, to recognize patterns that transcend data analysis, and to distinguish between information and wisdom. In a world where AI can process vast amounts of information instantly, humans become valuable for their ability to ask better questions, challenge assumptions, and recognize when quantitative analysis misses qualitative dimensions that matter.

This discernment develops through experience, reflection, and exposure to diverse perspectives that help us understand the limitations of any single way of understanding complex situations.

Empathy extends far beyond emotional intelligence to encompass cultural understanding, historical awareness, and the capacity to imagine how decisions affect stakeholders who aren't present in the room. As AI systems become better at analyzing behavior patterns and predicting responses, humans become more valuable for understanding the deeper motivations, fears, and aspirations that shape how people experience change.

Narrative Intelligence involves the ability to help others make meaning from complexity, to frame challenges and opportunities in ways that inspire engagement rather than overwhelm, and to connect current decisions to larger stories about identity, purpose, and possibility.

The most effective leaders aren't necessarily those with the best analytical skills, but those who can help their teams understand how current struggles connect to larger purposes, how temporary setbacks fit into longer trajectories of growth, and how individual contributions matter to collective success.

Ethical Calibration means developing moral imagination that can navigate the complex trade-offs that emerge when technological capability outpaces wisdom about how that capability should be used. This involves asking not just "Can we do this?" but "Should we do this?" and "What are the broader implications of this choice?"

Curiosity represents perhaps the most important mindset for professional futureproofing—the capacity to approach uncertainty with excitement rather than anxiety, to treat challenges as learning opportunities rather than threats, and to maintain beginner's mind even in domains where we have extensive expertise.

Curiosity prevents the intellectual rigidity that makes professionals obsolete when circumstances change. It fuels the continuous learning that keeps skills relevant and the creative thinking that discovers new applications for existing knowledge.

The next professional credential won't be a platform certification or technical badge—it will be **presence**: the ability to show up with integrity, imagination, and insight to whatever challenges emerge. That quality of presence can't be automated, outsourced, or made obsolete by technological advancement.

IV. Working Soulfully with Intelligent Tools

The professionals of tomorrow will not simply "use AI" in the way previous generations used calculators or word processors. They will **collaborate** with intelligent systems in ongoing relationships that require emotional intelligence, cultural sensitivity, and ethical awareness alongside technical proficiency.

This collaboration involves several key dimensions:

Treating systems as feedback partners rather than output engines means engaging AI in iterative dialogue rather than one-way command-response interactions. Effective professionals learn to share context, ask clarifying questions, and provide feedback that helps intelligent systems understand not just what they want to accomplish, but why it matters and how it connects to larger purposes.

In my own manuscript development work, I don't simply request AI assistance with editing or organization. I share the cultural context that shapes my writing choices, the audience I'm hoping to reach, and the transformation I hope to facilitate through my work. This context helps the AI provide suggestions that serve my deeper intentions rather than just optimizing for generic effectiveness.

Designing workflows that include emotional and ethical checks ensures that efficiency gains from AI collaboration don't come at the expense of human wisdom about relationships, values, and long-term consequences. This might involve building pauses into automated processes, creating opportunities for human review of AI recommendations, and maintaining accountability for decisions even when they're supported by intelligent analysis.

Customizing technology to reflect personal brand voice and values rather than accepting generic AI assistance that might improve technical quality while diluting authentic expression. Professionals must learn to train AI systems to understand their unique communication styles, cultural backgrounds, and value commitments.

Creating rituals that prompt reflection rather than just automation helps maintain awareness of why work matters, not just how efficiently it can be completed. These rituals might include starting projects with intention-setting, ending work sessions with gratitude or reflection, and regularly reviewing whether AI assistance is serving deeper purposes or just creating busy work.

In my facilitation practice, AI now supports various aspects of innovation sessions—clustering ideas, suggesting reframes, identifying patterns—but I've developed rituals that ensure technological assistance enhances rather than replaces the relational foundations that make breakthrough thinking possible.

Before introducing AI tools, I always begin with human connection activities that help participants understand their shared purposes and develop trust with each other. During AI-assisted activities, I maintain awareness of group energy and emotional dynamics that algorithms can't read. After sessions, I include reflection time that helps teams understand what they learned about collaboration, not just what they produced.

The goal isn't seamless human-AI integration, but **purposeful conversation with technology** that leverages artificial capabilities while preserving human agency, cultural authenticity, and ethical awareness.

V. Identity Anchoring: Staying Human in Intelligent Work

When machines mirror our tone, cadence, and choices with increasing sophistication, professionals must develop stronger rather than weaker anchors to their authentic identity, cultural heritage, and core values. The risk isn't that AI will replace human workers, but that human workers will gradually lose touch with the distinctively human qualities that make their contributions irreplaceable.

Professional identity anchoring involves three essential elements:

Voice represents the unique language, perspective, and communication style that reflects your cultural background, personal experience, and professional expertise. This isn't just about vocabulary or grammar—it's about the underlying worldview, value system, and way of understanding human experience that shapes how you frame problems, describe solutions, and relate to others.

Developing authentic professional voice requires understanding what makes your perspective distinctive: What experiences have shaped your worldview? What cultural traditions influence your approach to relationships and problem-solving? What values guide your decisions when pressures mount and compromise becomes tempting?

Values encompass the non-negotiable principles that guide decision-making even when market pressures, technological possibilities, or social expectations suggest different choices. These values serve as both compass and constraint, providing direction during uncertainty while establishing boundaries around what kinds of success are worth pursuing.

Professional values become more rather than less important in AI-enhanced work environments, because intelligent systems excel at optimizing for defined metrics but cannot provide the moral imagination that determines what should be optimized and at what cost.

Vision connects daily work activities to larger purposes that extend beyond immediate job responsibilities to encompass contribution to communities, industries, and social causes that matter. This vision provides motivation during difficult periods and helps maintain perspective when short-term pressures threaten to overwhelm long-term purposes.

Professional vision isn't just personal ambition or career goals—it's understanding of how your unique combination of skills, experience, and values can serve needs that extend beyond your immediate self-interest.

One client drafted: "I am a strategist who listens with data, learns through design, and leads with story. I use intelligent systems to expand my capacity for analysis while maintaining responsibility for wisdom and judgment that serves human flourishing."

That statement became her North Star for making decisions about which AI tools to adopt, how to structure her workflows, and what kinds of projects aligned with her evolving professional identity.

Identity anchoring isn't about resistance to change, but about **integration of innovation with inheritance**—allowing technological capability to enhance rather than replace the cultural wisdom, emotional intelligence, and moral imagination that make human contributions irreplaceable.

VI. Building Adaptive Workflows

Adapting to intelligent tools requires more than learning to use new software—it demands fundamental redesign of how work gets structured, how decisions get made, and how value gets created through the intersection of human wisdom and artificial capability.

Reflection Intervals represent perhaps the most important innovation in AI-enhanced workflows. Traditional productivity approaches emphasize continuous action and rapid iteration. But soulful work with intelligent systems requires scheduled time for discernment, meaning-making, and values alignment that prevents technological momentum from overwhelming human judgment.

These intervals might include daily check-ins about whether AI assistance is serving intended purposes, weekly reviews of whether workflow changes are improving both efficiency and job satisfaction, and monthly evaluations of whether technological collaboration is strengthening or weakening professional relationships and cultural connections.

Emotion Maps track engagement, trust, energy, and satisfaction throughout AI-enhanced work processes, ensuring that productivity gains don't come at the expense of psychological well-being or authentic self-expression. Many professionals report feeling more efficient but less fulfilled when they begin using AI assistance extensively, suggesting that emotional considerations deserve explicit attention in workflow design.

Hybrid Partnership Models deliberately combine human review with machine suggestions, ensuring that efficiency gains from automation don't eliminate opportunities for learning, relationship building, and serendipitous discovery that often emerge from less efficient but more exploratory approaches to work.

Rather than maximizing AI automation, these models identify which aspects of work benefit from human attention—even when machines could handle them more efficiently—because the human engagement serves purposes beyond immediate task completion.

Narrative Markers use story checkpoints throughout projects to ensure that momentum remains aligned with mission, that activity serves deeper purposes, and that busy work doesn't disguise lack of meaningful progress toward goals that matter.

In one consulting engagement, a client team was using AI to accelerate product development cycles dramatically. While technically impressive, team members reported feeling disconnected from their work and uncertain about whether faster development was actually serving customer needs more effectively.

We redesigned their workflow to include "Story Pauses"—brief reflections at key project milestones where the team considered how their technical progress connected to user experiences, organizational mission, and personal satisfaction with their professional contribution.

These pauses revealed that rapid iteration was generating impressive feature lists but losing sight of user experience coherence and authentic value creation. The team chose to slow down their AI-assisted development in favor of more thoughtful integration that served long-term success rather than just short-term productivity metrics.

The key insight was that **workflow evolution must serve human flourishing rather than just technological optimization**. The most adaptive professionals learn to leverage AI capabilities while maintaining agency over their own work experience and authentic contribution to meaningful purposes.

VII. Navigating Ethical Transformation

Futureproof professionals don't just automate ethically—they lead ethically in environments where technological capability often outpaces wisdom about how that capability should be used. This leadership requires developing comfort with slowing down efficient processes when ethical reflection is needed, confidence in questioning AI recommendations when they conflict with human values, and skill in facilitating difficult conversations about trade-offs between optimization and integrity.

Auditing assumptions behind AI systems becomes a core professional responsibility rather than a specialized technical skill. Every professional who collaborates with intelligent systems must develop literacy about how those systems work, what biases they might carry, and what values they embed through their design and training.

This doesn't require becoming a data scientist or AI engineer, but it does require asking good questions: Whose perspectives shaped the training data? What cultural assumptions are embedded in the algorithms? How does the system define success or failure? What voices might be missing from its knowledge base?

Holding space for emotional feedback ensures that efficiency gains from technological collaboration don't eliminate opportunities for team members to express concerns, confusion, or values conflicts that emerge as AI becomes more prevalent in workplace culture.

Many organizations implement AI tools quickly and measure success through productivity metrics without creating opportunities for workers to process the psychological and social implications of changing relationships with technology.

Advocating for inclusive training models means using influence within organizations and professional networks to ensure that AI systems serve diverse communities rather than replicating existing patterns of exclusion or discrimination.

Professionals must develop **ethical literacy** that includes understanding how data flows affect trust relationships, knowing when to challenge AI suggestions based on values rather than just accuracy, and maintaining awareness of how technological choices affect stakeholders who aren't present in immediate decision-making processes.

I work with leadership teams to develop "Ethical Decision-Making Protocols" that help them navigate complex situations where AI recommendations conflict with organizational values, where efficiency pressures compete with fairness considerations, and where short-term gains might create long-term trust problems.

These protocols include questions like: "Who benefits from this AI-recommended approach, and who might be harmed?" "How does this decision align with our stated organizational values?" "What would we want others to know about how we made this choice?"

The soul of futureproofing lies in **moral courage**—the willingness to pause efficient processes when ethical reflection is needed, to question technological authority when it conflicts with human wisdom, and to advocate for approaches that serve human dignity even when alternatives might provide competitive advantage.

VIII. Creating Emotional Resilience in Intelligent Teams

Intelligent systems change the emotional terrain of teamwork in ways that require conscious attention and proactive design. The speed and scale at which AI can process information and generate options can create cognitive overwhelm. The efficiency of automated processes can reduce opportunities for informal relationship building that has traditionally sustained team cohesion.

Building emotional resilience in AI-enhanced teams requires understanding these dynamics and designing interventions that preserve the human elements that make collaborative work sustainable and meaningful:

Emotional Checkpoints create structured opportunities for team members to share how AI collaboration is affecting their sense of agency, creativity, and connection to their work. These might include brief check-ins during meetings, anonymous feedback systems, or regular team reflection sessions focused on the human experience of technological change.

Many teams implement AI tools without creating space for workers to process the psychological adjustment required when familiar work patterns change rapidly.

AI-assisted tone monitoring can help teams recognize when technological efficiency is creating communication patterns that feel impersonal or overwhelming. Some AI systems can track email sentiment, meeting participation patterns, and communication frequency to identify when team dynamics might need attention.

But this monitoring must be transparent and consensual, focused on supporting team health rather than surveilling individual performance.

Reflection practices help teams distinguish between technical problems that AI can solve and human dynamics that require relational attention. Questions might include: "Did our AI assistance enhance or diminish our connection as a team?" "Are we maintaining space for intuition and creativity alongside data analysis?" "How are we ensuring that everyone's voice remains valued as AI capabilities expand?"

I helped one technology company address mounting tension between team members who embraced AI assistance enthusiastically and those who felt overwhelmed or displaced by rapid technological adoption. Rather than forcing uniform adoption or allowing division to persist, we created "Integration Circles" where team members could share their experiences and concerns about AI collaboration.

These circles revealed that resistance often stemmed not from fear of technology but from lack of choice about how AI got integrated into workflows. Team members wanted to maintain agency over their technological relationships rather than having AI assistance imposed through top-down decisions.

The solution involved creating individual choice about AI adoption timelines, providing training that honored different learning styles and comfort levels, and maintaining alternative workflows for team members who preferred different approaches to their professional practice.

The result was increased rather than decreased AI adoption, because people felt empowered to choose how technology served their work rather than feeling coerced into accepting predetermined approaches.

Emotional resilience in intelligent teams requires **honoring the human need for agency, meaning, and connection** even as technological capabilities expand. The goal isn't eliminating emotional challenge from technological change, but ensuring that teams have the support and resources needed to navigate that change while maintaining their essential humanity and collaborative capacity.

IX. Designing a Soulful Professional Development Plan

Traditional professional development focuses on accumulating credentials, attending training programs, and acquiring measurable competencies that can be documented on résumés and evaluated through performance reviews. But developing for an intelligent future requires a different approach—one that emphasizes identity evolution, values clarification, and capacity building that serves both individual flourishing and collective contribution to meaningful purposes.

Soulful professional development integrates five essential dimensions:

Voice Development involves discovering and articulating your unique perspective, communication style, and cultural contribution to professional communities. This isn't about personal branding or marketing yourself, but about understanding what makes your viewpoint distinctive and how to express that distinctiveness authentically across different contexts and technological platforms.

Voice development might include reflecting on formative experiences that shaped your worldview, identifying cultural traditions that influence your approach to problem-solving, practicing communication across different audiences while maintaining authentic expression, and developing confidence in expressing perspectives that might differ from dominant professional norms.

Values Integration ensures that professional choices remain aligned with deeper principles even as circumstances change and new opportunities emerge. This involves not just identifying what you believe, but developing practices that help you apply those beliefs consistently across complex professional situations.

Skill Development remains important but should focus on capabilities that complement rather than compete with AI strengths. This includes emotional intelligence, cultural competency, systems thinking, ethical reasoning, creative problem-solving, and facilitation skills that leverage rather than resist technological enhancement.

Rather than trying to become better at tasks that AI can perform more efficiently, professionals should focus on developing uniquely human capabilities that become more valuable as AI handles routine cognitive work.

Relationship Building recognizes that professional success increasingly depends on the ability to collaborate across diverse teams, communicate effectively with stakeholders who have different backgrounds and priorities, and build trust relationships that can withstand technological disruption and organizational change.

Vision Cultivation connects individual professional development to larger purposes that extend beyond career advancement to encompass contribution to communities, industries, and social causes that matter.

This dimension helps maintain motivation during difficult periods, provides direction for making choices among competing opportunities, and ensures that professional growth serves not just individual success but collective flourishing.

Rather than collecting random skills or credentials, these maps help professionals understand how their individual development can serve larger purposes while building the capacities most needed for thriving in intelligent work environments.

X. The Role of Story in Career Shaping

Narrative helps professionals connect the dots between past experiences, current choices, and future possibilities in ways that create coherence and motivation even when external circumstances change rapidly. Career development in the intelligence age requires understanding your professional journey not as a series of jobs or accomplishments, but as an evolving story about how you're developing and deploying your unique capacities in service of purposes that matter to you.

Career Narrative Maps help professionals understand the thematic threads that connect different experiences, the values that have guided major decisions, and the patterns of growth that suggest future directions worth exploring.

These maps go beyond chronological résumés to explore questions like: What kinds of challenges consistently energize you? What values have guided your major career decisions? How has your understanding of meaningful work evolved over time? What patterns of growth suggest future possibilities you haven't yet considered?

AI-assisted story refinement can help professionals articulate their career narratives more clearly, identify patterns they might not have recognized, and develop language that communicates their distinctive value proposition effectively.

AI tools can suggest alternative ways to frame professional experiences, help identify skills and achievements that might be taken for granted, and provide feedback on how career stories might resonate with different audiences.

But the essential work of meaning-making—understanding why particular experiences were significant, how they connect to larger purposes, and what they reveal about future directions—remains fundamentally human.

Values-based positioning helps professionals communicate not just what they can do, but why they choose to do it and how their work serves purposes larger than immediate job responsibilities.

Instead of generic functional descriptions, values-based positioning helps professionals articulate the distinctive combination of skills, experience, and values they bring to challenges that matter to them.

One client transformed his professional positioning from "project management specialist" to "relationship architect who builds spaces where clarity meets care." This shift, supported by AI assistance in refining language and testing different phrasings, became his differentiator in competitive job markets.

The narrative approach reflected not just what he did professionally, but why it mattered to him and how it served the human dimensions of organizational success that often get overlooked in efficiency-focused work cultures.

Story becomes the bridge between skill and soul, connecting technical capabilities to human purposes in ways that make professional development more than career advancement—transforming it into identity evolution that serves both individual flourishing and collective contribution to meaningful work.

XI. Measuring Success in Soulful Terms

Traditional professional success metrics—salary growth, title advancement, productivity measures, performance ratings—provide important feedback about career progression but often miss the deeper dimensions that determine whether work feels meaningful and sustainable over time.

Futureproof professionals must develop expanded definitions of success that include qualitative dimensions alongside quantitative achievements:

Impact Resonance measures whether your work creates the kinds of changes you actually care about, not just changes that can be easily quantified. This might involve collecting stories about how your contributions affected real people, tracking whether projects create lasting value rather than just immediate results, and maintaining awareness of how your work ripples through communities and relationships.

Rather than just counting outputs, impact resonance asks: Are you solving problems that matter? Are you creating value that endures? Are you contributing to changes that align with your deepest values about what makes life better for others?

Learning Velocity tracks not just what new skills you acquire, but how quickly you can adapt to changing circumstances, integrate new information with existing knowledge, and apply learning in creative ways to novel challenges.

In rapidly changing professional environments, the ability to learn and adapt often matters more than any specific knowledge or skill set. Learning velocity includes curiosity, intellectual humility, and the capacity to remain a beginner even in domains where you have extensive expertise.

Relationship Quality evaluates whether your professional relationships are deepening and multiplying in ways that create mutual support, collaborative opportunity, and shared learning. This includes not just networking quantity but relationship depth—the extent to which you're known and trusted by people whose values align with yours.

Quality relationships provide both support during difficult periods and collaboration opportunities that accelerate professional growth while serving purposes larger than individual advancement.

Authenticity Integration assesses whether your professional persona feels aligned with your personal values, cultural identity, and deepest sense of purpose. This dimension recognizes that sustainable success requires coherence between who you are and how you show up professionally.

Regenerative Capacity tracks whether your work creates energy and enthusiasm or depletes and exhausts you over time. Sustainable professional development requires approaches that strengthen rather than diminish your capacity for creativity, relationship, and contribution.

I help clients develop "Holistic Success Dashboards" that integrate these qualitative measures with traditional professional metrics, creating accountability for the full spectrum of professional thriving rather than just measurable achievement.

These dashboards help professionals make career decisions based on comprehensive consideration of what success means to them, rather than defaulting to external expectations or societal definitions that might not align with their authentic values and aspirations.

XII. Looking Forward: The Professional as Cultural Steward

As artificial intelligence automates increasing amounts of routine cognitive work, human professionals become more valuable for capabilities that resist automation: cultural wisdom, emotional intelligence, ethical reasoning, creative problem-solving, and the ability to create meaning from complexity.

But these capabilities aren't just individual assets—they're **cultural inheritance** that professionals have responsibility to preserve, develop, and transmit to future generations of workers who will face even more complex relationships between human and artificial intelligence.

Cultural Stewardship means understanding your professional development not just as individual advancement but as contribution to preserving and evolving valuable human capacities that societies need to thrive.

This might involve mentoring younger professionals who are navigating AI-enhanced work environments, advocating for organizational policies that honor human dignity alongside efficiency, and maintaining practices that preserve cultural wisdom alongside technological innovation.

Wisdom Transmission recognizes that your accumulated experience with navigating technological change, maintaining authenticity in digital environments, and integrating efficiency with meaning provides valuable guidance for others facing similar challenges.

Rather than hoarding insights that helped you succeed, wisdom transmission involves sharing learning generously while remaining humble about the limitations of any individual's experience and perspective.

Legacy Building connects current professional choices to longer-term impacts on industries, communities, and cultures that will inherit the technological systems and work practices you help create today.

This perspective helps maintain motivation for making thoughtful rather than expedient choices, even when ethical approaches require more effort or generate less immediate reward than alternatives focused purely on efficiency or profit.

The professional of the future becomes a **cultural steward** who uses technological capability to serve human flourishing, who maintains space for wisdom alongside intelligence, and who ensures that progress honors rather than erases the cultural traditions and human values that make work meaningful across generations.

You are not preparing to be useful—you are preparing to be irreplaceable. You are not adapting to survive change—you are evolving to steward it. You are not futureproofing against uncertainty—you are developing wisdom to navigate it with grace.

The future will be shaped by professionals who understand that their deepest value lies not in competing with machines, but in bringing distinctively human capacities to challenges that become more rather than less complex as artificial intelligence advances.

CHAPTER 9

Publishing Wisdom: The Human Voice in the Machine

I. From Message to Movement

"Publishing isn't just about sharing content. It's about shaping consciousness."

Publishing has transformed from permanence to flow, from ceremony to stream. My grandfather understood the weight of words committed to form—each letter carved or written with the knowledge that what he created would endure. His workshop motto, "Built to Last," reflected this understanding that creation carries responsibility for legacy.

Today's publishing flows across platforms in real-time, mediated by algorithms that amplify, distort, or bury our words faster than we can comprehend. We publish continuously—posts that appear and vanish, updates that scroll past unread, messages filtered through systems we don't understand.

Yet beneath this technological transformation lies a crucial question: Does our wisdom still lead? In a landscape increasingly shaped by algorithmic optimization, is the human voice still audible? Are we shaping consciousness through our words, or merely feeding content into systems that reshape consciousness according to logics we can't control?

The future doesn't need more noise—it needs more meaning. And the responsibility for ensuring published wisdom serves human flourishing lies with those who choose words carefully, publish with intention, and remember that every piece of content carries potential to shape how others understand themselves and their possibilities.

II. Reframing Publishing: Wisdom as Living Asset

Traditional publishing treated content as finished product—books and articles that remained static while readers encountered them. Today, wisdom breathes across multiple platforms simultaneously:

Dynamic platforms enable ongoing conversation between creators and audiences, where ideas evolve through dialogue rather than remaining fixed. Podcasts, blogs, and social media allow iterative development but risk fragmenting complex insights into digestible pieces that lose coherence.

Algorithmic mediation surfaces our work to unintended audiences with interpretive frameworks we never anticipated. Ideas travel through recommendation engines that may distort meaning or reach readers who lack necessary background for understanding.

AI-generated content can mimic human style and synthesize ideas, producing compelling content that resembles insight without the lived experience that traditionally gave published wisdom its authority.

In this environment, publishing requires strategic stewardship—ongoing responsibility for how ideas travel through communities and influence understanding across time and culture. Publishing isn't about completing tasks efficiently, but about participating in conversations that shape what it means to be human.

Speaking with authenticity means maintaining clear connection to voice, values, and cultural inheritance even when AI assistance offers improvements that might enhance technical proficiency while diminishing personal distinctiveness.

Protecting nuance involves resisting pressure to simplify complex ideas into formats that travel easily but lose subtlety and ambiguity that often contain the most important insights.

Honoring tone requires awareness of emotional and relational dimensions that shape how ideas get received and applied—the same information can inspire or discourage depending on how it's crafted.

Aligning method with message ensures publishing practices reflect content values. If your work advocates human dignity, your publishing should demonstrate respect for readers' intelligence and cultural backgrounds.

III. Intelligent Technology in the Publishing Process

AI can support writers throughout the publishing journey when approached as collaborative partner rather than replacement:

Ideation and Development involves AI suggesting themes based on previous writing, cultural conversations, and audience needs. Systems can identify content gaps your perspective might fill and propose connections between separately explored ideas.

Structural Organization represents AI's most reliable contribution—suggesting outlines that balance clarity with emotional engagement, identifying logical sequences, and recognizing patterns that resonate with different reader expectations.

Tone Calibration helps content resonate with specific audiences while preserving authentic voice. This might include adjusting formality levels or suggesting metaphors that bridge cultural differences.

Research Integration allows AI to identify relevant sources, synthesize information, and suggest citations that strengthen arguments without overwhelming readers.

Platform Optimization helps understand how content might perform across different channels and what modifications could improve discoverability without compromising integrity.

The key is providing rich context about values, cultural background, and intended impact. Quality AI collaboration depends on depth of human input about purpose, audience, and desired transformation.

IV. The Soulful Publishing Framework

Effective publishing in the intelligence age requires intentional attention to five essential dimensions:

Purpose Clarity asks foundational questions: What matters here, and why? What transformation do you hope to facilitate? What conversation do you want to join? This prevents "content drift"—publishing without clear intention in response to platform pressures rather than serving deeper purposes.

Voice Authenticity ensures published work reflects cultural background, personal experience, and distinctive perspective rather than optimized professional communication. This involves preserving linguistic patterns and cultural references that might seem "inefficient" but provide authentic connection to inherited wisdom.

Structural Integrity means organizing content to invite meaningful engagement rather than efficient consumption. This includes emotional pacing that prevents reader fatigue and narrative architecture that connects insights to larger frameworks of meaning.

Emotional Resonance recognizes readers as complex beings experiencing relationship with ideas, authors, and communities through content. This requires understanding audience fears, aspirations, and life circumstances that shape reception.

Impact Integration asks whether published content creates changes you actually care about—collecting stories about real effects, tracking lasting value, and maintaining awareness of how ideas ripple through communities over time.

V. Protecting Heritage and Identity

One major risk in AI-assisted publishing is gradual erosion of cultural distinctiveness. Intelligent systems often suggest improvements that make content more accessible while eliminating the cultural specificity that gives authentic voices their power.

Cultural Communication Patterns include natural speech rhythms and emotional builds that reflect how ideas are shared within specific communities. Italian-American narrative often involves circular storytelling where meaning emerges through layered repetition rather than direct linear progression.

Narrative Traditions carry specific cultural meanings that resist translation into universal symbols. When I write about Sunday dinner conversations, I'm invoking entire systems of relationship and cultural transmission, not just describing family gatherings.

Emotional Expression Patterns reflect different cultural approaches to vulnerability, authority, and relationship-building. Some traditions emphasize indirect communication, while others prefer direct confrontation—both deserve technological support.

To preserve cultural authenticity:

- Annotate AI corrections with cultural intent

- Create heritage glossaries explaining cultural symbols
- Set boundaries around sacred cultural elements
- Maintain community accountability for authentic expression

VI. Platform Consciousness: Where You Publish Matters

Each platform carries embedded assumptions about communication, audience expectations, and values. Choosing where to publish has become as important as choosing what to publish.

Tone expectations vary dramatically—LinkedIn rewards professional optimism while academic platforms value critical analysis. Understanding these expectations helps match content to appropriate environments.

Audience attention patterns differ significantly—Twitter users expect brief insights while Medium readers seek deeper exploration. Newsletter subscribers want regular communication while book readers expect comprehensive treatment.

Algorithmic systems determine content visibility based on engagement patterns that may not align with deeper purposes. Understanding these mechanics helps serve authentic goals rather than gaming systems.

Platform consciousness means:

- Aligning message with medium capabilities
- Assessing values coherence between platform and content

- Evaluating whether platforms serve intended audiences
- Building long-term relationships rather than maximizing metrics

VII. Emotional and Ethical Calibration

Publishing in the intelligence age requires editorial consciousness that extends beyond accuracy to include emotional impact and ethical implications.

Emotional Editing involves conscious attention to psychological experience created for readers. Does content inspire hope without unrealistic expectations? Does it acknowledge difficulty without creating despair? Does it challenge growth without attacking current understanding?

Ethical Calibration extends responsibility beyond individual readers to broader social implications. How might ideas be misinterpreted? What voices are missing? How does content affect power dynamics within reached communities?

This includes:

- Cultural sensitivity review
- Power dynamics awareness
- Harm prevention protocols
- Integrity maintenance

VIII. Publishing for Transformation

Attention economy creates pressure for engagement and thought leadership positioning. But transformation-oriented publishing asks different questions:

Instead of "What will get attention?" ask "What understanding would genuinely help people navigate challenges?"

Instead of "What topics are trending?" ask "What insights from experience might spare others unnecessary struggle?"

Instead of "How can I position expertise?" ask "How can I serve learning and growth of communities I care about?"

Reader Experience Design involves conscious attention to the journey created for people engaging your work—not just information architecture but emotional arc and practical application opportunities.

Community Catalyst Publishing recognizes that valuable content often serves as starting point for conversation rather than final word, helping communities think together more effectively.

AI can assist through impact tracking beyond engagement metrics, feedback integration that identifies genuine reader value, and ethical impact assessment that reveals unintended consequences.

IX. Legacy Publishing: Co-Creating Meaning Across Time

Some publishing work involves capturing wisdom that transcends immediate contexts to serve communities across extended time periods:

Collaborative Heritage Documentation uses AI assistance to help families and organizations preserve stories and cultural wisdom that might otherwise be lost as older generations pass away.

Cross-Cultural Wisdom Translation involves AI capability to help preserve cultural knowledge across language barriers while maintaining authenticity and emotional resonance.

Future-Facing Wisdom Letters invite current leaders to articulate learning that might serve future decision-makers facing challenges we can't imagine.

Legacy publishing becomes cultural inheritance when it successfully transmits not just information but wisdom about carrying forward values and insights that serve human flourishing across changing circumstances.

X. Building Systems for Soulful Publishing

Sustainable meaningful publishing requires systems supporting reflection, authenticity, and community connection:

Rhythm and Pacing help maintain consistency without sacrificing quality, involving seasonal publishing rhythms aligned with creative cycles and adequate reflection time between development and sharing.

Values Integration Protocols ensure publishing choices remain aligned with deeper principles even when market pressures suggest different approaches.

Community Feedback Loops create structured opportunities for readers to provide input improving both individual pieces and overall strategy.

Cultural Authenticity Safeguards protect against gradual erosion of distinctive voice through technological optimization.

Legacy Documentation Practices ensure published work contributes to larger bodies of wisdom serving communities across extended time periods.

XI. Looking Forward: Publishing as Cultural Stewardship

As AI systems become more sophisticated in generating human-like content, the challenge isn't competing with artificial efficiency but developing the distinctively human elements that make published work transformative rather than just informative.

The evolution of authentic voice requires conscious development of cultural specificity, emotional intelligence from lived experience, moral imagination from ethical wrestling, and creative insight from unpredictable intersections of diverse experiences.

Collaborative publishing models leverage AI efficiency while preserving human wisdom—AI handles research synthesis while humans provide cultural context, or hybrid creation where AI generates options that humans select based on deeper purposes.

Cultural preservation responsibilities become urgent as AI systems risk homogenizing diverse communication approaches. Publishers from non-dominant backgrounds must maintain distinctive patterns and ensure AI serves rather than erases cultural diversity.

Future-oriented accountability recognizes that published content shapes cultural conversations affecting real people's lives across extended time periods.

The future of human voice in intelligent publishing will be determined by collective choices about integrating technological capability with cultural wisdom, preserving authentic expression while leveraging AI assistance, and ensuring published work serves human flourishing rather than just algorithmic optimization.

The essential questions include: Does this work honor cultural traditions and experiences that gave birth to these insights? Does AI assistance enhance or compromise authentic voice? Are we serving communities better or just producing content more efficiently?

Let us approach every publication as opportunity to frame futures that honor both human heritage and artificial possibility, that serve both individual expression and community wisdom, that create both immediate value and long-term contribution to the ancient human project of transforming experience into wisdom through the sacred art of words that carry both information and soul.

CHAPTER 10

Designing Soulful Systems: Infrastructure for Meaningful Work

I. Beyond Platforms: The Soul of Design

"The best systems don't just work --- they care."

We've built dazzling technological infrastructure: cloud architectures spanning continents, collaboration platforms connecting global teams, real-time data pipelines processing millions of transactions, and AI systems analyzing patterns beyond human comprehension. Yet beneath this technical sophistication, many professionals report feeling exhausted, disconnected, and spiritually empty in their daily work.

The systems designed to liberate us from routine often feel like digital treadmills demanding constant motion without meaningful progress. Platforms meant to enhance collaboration sometimes create barriers to authentic human connection. Tools built to amplify capabilities occasionally make us feel more like data points than human beings.

My grandfather, a craftsman who worked with hand tools, understood something we've forgotten. Every tool in his workshop was selected not just for capability but for how it felt in his hands, how it connected him to his work, and how it supported the quality of attention that meaningful craftsmanship requires. His workspace was organized not for maximum efficiency but for flow that supported both practical accomplishment and spiritual satisfaction.

This wisdom about systemic design becomes more relevant as we create digital infrastructure mediating increasing proportions of human work and relationship. Soulful system design doesn't ask only how well something works—it asks what kind of world it builds, what relationships it enables, and what kinds of humans it calls forth through daily interaction.

II. Systems as Cultural Mirrors

Every system reflects the values, assumptions, and cultural patterns of its builders, whether conscious or unconscious. The infrastructure we create shapes daily experience for everyone who interacts with it, encoding particular approaches to relationship, authority, communication, and meaning-making into work itself.

I've worked with organizations whose platforms were technically sophisticated yet culturally barren—systems processing tasks flawlessly while making employees feel unseen and uninvited to contribute their full humanity. These platforms reflected assumptions about what matters: speed over reflection, standardization over diversity, individual productivity over collective relationship.

The cultural code embedded in infrastructure operates at multiple levels:

Power Flow Architecture determines who makes decisions, whose voices get amplified, and whose concerns receive attention. Traditional hierarchical systems may not serve contemporary challenges requiring distributed intelligence and collaborative problem-solving.

Value Amplification Systems shape which behaviors get rewarded and contributions recognized. Every tracked metric signals organizational priorities, influencing behavior beyond explicit policies.

Communication Assumptions reflect cultural expectations about directness, decision-making, relationship building, and emotion's role in professional interaction. Systems designed by dominant cultural groups often embed patterns that feel alienating to users from different traditions.

Attention Architecture shapes what information surfaces, when interruptions occur, and how cognitive resources get allocated throughout the workday, profoundly affecting user experience while remaining invisible.

In one strategy retreat, a team realized their feedback portal had no open-ended fields or emotional expression mechanisms—only numerical ratings and predetermined categories. The AI couldn't interpret qualitative feedback, so designers eliminated opportunities for nuanced human input. Over time, employees stopped sharing meaningful feedback because the system couldn't receive what they needed to communicate.

This led to fundamental redesign including narrative feedback options, cultural liaison roles, and AI training that could recognize and preserve emotional and cultural nuance rather than eliminating it.

Soulful system design asks: What assumptions shape our infrastructure? Do our tools mirror care or control? Do they invite authentic participation or demand conformity to algorithmic expectations?

III. The Architecture of Soulful Systems

Through decades of helping organizations humanize their technology, I've identified five essential dimensions that determine whether digital infrastructure supports or undermines meaningful work:

Purpose Clarity ensures every component serves articulated intentions extending beyond functionality to encompass human experience and cultural values the infrastructure should support. This prevents "feature drift"—accumulating capabilities that seem useful in isolation but don't serve coherent vision.

Empathy Integration means designing systems recognizing and responding to human emotional needs, cultural differences, and varying circumstances affecting technology engagement. Empathetic systems understand users as complex beings whose needs and capabilities fluctuate based on factors pure functionality cannot address.

Transparency Architecture makes system logic visible and comprehensible, enabling genuine understanding of decision-making processes and maintaining meaningful user agency. Rather than hiding complexity, transparent systems help users develop mental models supporting collaborative relationship.

Adaptability Design ensures systems evolve with changing human values, organizational cultures, and community needs rather than locking users into predetermined approaches. This includes learning mechanisms, customization options, and upgrade pathways preserving user agency.

Ritualization Support recognizes meaningful work often requires ceremonial elements—beginnings and endings, reflection pauses, transition acknowledgment—creating psychological coherence and spiritual satisfaction alongside task completion.

This framework helps teams assess whether technological infrastructure honors human agency, creates space for authentic expression, and strengthens rather than weakens cultural and relational foundations making work sustainable.

IV. Designing Interfaces That Honor Humanity

Creating systems supporting authentic visibility rather than superficial surveillance requires design approaches honoring human complexity, cultural diversity, and recognition that helps people feel genuinely seen.

Language That Invites Rather Than Commands represents fundamental shift toward soulful interface design. Traditional systems use imperative language treating users as subordinates: "Enter data," "Select option." Soulful interfaces use invitational language recognizing user agency: "Would you like to share thoughts?" "What option feels aligned with your goals?"

Cultural Responsiveness involves interface elements adapting to diverse communication styles, aesthetic preferences, and relationship patterns without forcing users to abandon cultural identities for platform conformity.

Emotional Calibration means interfaces recognizing and responding to user emotional states with appropriate sensitivity, offering different support types based on stress levels or expressed preferences.

Agency-Preserving Assistance provides support enhancing rather than replacing human decision-making, ensuring technological assistance builds user confidence in their judgment and capability.

Time Consciousness recognizes users exist within natural rhythms affecting their capacity for different types of technological engagement.

Dignity-Preserving Error Handling treats mistakes as learning opportunities rather than failures, providing guidance building confidence when users struggle with complexity.

I worked with a healthcare organization redesigning their patient portal after discovering clinical efficiency was creating emotional distance undermining patient trust. The redesigned system included personalized tone adaptation, cultural sensitivity options, emotional recognition and response, and celebration of health milestones.

The result was improved patient satisfaction and better health outcomes, as patients felt more comfortable sharing complete information and following treatment recommendations when communication felt respectful and personally relevant.

V. Intelligent Systems as Ritual Partners

Traditional automation treats work as purely functional activity without regard for psychological, cultural, or spiritual dimensions making work meaningful. Intelligent systems can support ritual elements helping humans maintain connection to purpose, community, and values.

Rhythm Recognition and Support involves AI learning individual and team energy patterns, offering suggestions aligning with natural human rhythms rather than demanding consistent mechanical performance.

Transition Rituals help humans navigate psychological shifts between different work types or responsibility levels. AI can offer meditation prompts between meetings or gratitude practices at project completion.

Community Recognition and Celebration uses AI to identify moments when achievements deserve acknowledgment, ensuring meaningful accomplishments don't get lost in momentum toward next tasks.

Values Alignment Check-ins provide regular opportunities for individuals and teams to reflect on whether current work serves stated values and deeper purposes.

Sacred Pause Integration creates opportunities for stillness and reflection allowing deeper wisdom to emerge and guide subsequent action.

I helped a nonprofit embed "Wisdom Practices" into their project management system—AI-assisted prompts appearing at transition points helping staff pause for reflection: "You've been solving complex problems all week—what insights emerged that might help colleagues?" These prompts transformed routine review into meaningful reflection strengthening both individual development and organizational learning.

VI. Feedback Architecture: From Metrics to Meaning

Traditional feedback systems focus on performance measurement—productivity tracking, completion rates, outcome achievement. While valuable, these often miss qualitative dimensions determining whether work feels meaningful and teams remain healthy over time.

Multi-Dimensional Feedback Design captures both quantitative performance and qualitative experience information, creating complete pictures of how work gets done and what human experience it creates.

Narrative Integration invites users to share stories providing context for quantitative data: "What made this project meaningful?" "Where did you experience creative energy?" "What obstacles felt surmountable versus overwhelming?"

Emotional Pattern Recognition uses AI to identify stress indicators, energy fluctuations, and satisfaction patterns that might not appear through traditional monitoring but significantly affect well-being and team dynamics.

Cultural Resonance Tracking monitors whether systems and practices feel aligned with user cultural backgrounds, helping identify when efficiency optimizations create barriers for people from different traditions.

Wisdom Extraction Processes help organizations learn from both successes and failures, asking not just what happened but what was learned about approaches, cultural factors, and relational elements contributing to satisfying collaborations.

I worked with a technology company replacing traditional performance reviews with "Narrative Impact Maps"—quarterly reflections where AI helped explore both achievement and experience dimensions. Instead of focusing primarily on goal achievement, conversations explored questions like: "What work energized you most deeply?" "Where did you feel most authentic and effective?"

The AI clustered themes across team members, helping managers recognize patterns indicating cultural misalignment, resource needs, or development opportunities invisible through individual analysis. This resulted in more targeted support, better role alignment, and higher retention as people felt seen and valued for distinctive contributions.

VII. Systemic Bias: Naming and Designing Better

Bias isn't just interpersonal—it's infrastructural reality embedded through countless design decisions reflecting unconscious assumptions, cultural patterns, and privilege positions of system builders.

Recognition and Assessment involves systematic examination of who gets defaulted to what roles, what paths are pre-built versus requiring special requests, and which exceptions get treated as "edge cases" rather than legitimate needs.

Design Team Diversity ensures system builders include perspectives from affected communities, particularly voices from historically marginalized groups, with meaningful rather than tokenistic involvement in fundamental decisions.

Inclusive Use Case Development designs systems around the full spectrum of human experience rather than optimizing for dominant patterns and treating diversity as deviation.

Continuous Bias Monitoring uses AI to identify patterns indicating disparate impact on different user groups, even when unintended.

Community Accountability Integration includes mechanisms for affected communities to provide ongoing feedback about system impact and influence evolution based on lived experience.

I helped a hiring platform redesign their AI-assisted recruiting after discovering it recommended different interview processes for candidates with similar qualifications based on cultural name patterns and educational backgrounds. The solution involved training AI on more diverse success patterns, designing bias-reduced interview processes, and creating feedback loops monitoring hiring outcomes across demographic groups.

Rather than just adding diverse data, they fundamentally redesigned their approach including community health workers and cultural liaisons in development. The result was a system performing better across populations while helping providers recognize their own biases and develop more culturally responsive practices.

VIII. Embedding Emotional Intelligence into Infrastructure

Emotional intelligence in technological systems involves recognizing and responding to human emotional states in ways supporting rather than undermining psychological well-being and authentic relationship.

Stress Detection and Response involves systems recognizing indicators of user fatigue or emotional distress and responding with appropriate modifications to task load, communication style, or support resources.

Communication Tone Support helps users communicate effectively by offering suggestions improving clarity while preserving authentic expression, particularly during difficult conversations or cross-cultural communication.

Collaborative Climate Monitoring tracks team emotional dynamics over time, identifying patterns indicating growing tension, decreased psychological safety, or opportunities for celebration.

Individual Adaptation customizes system behavior based on user emotional patterns, communication preferences, and feedback about supportive versus overwhelming technological assistance.

Empathy Without Intrusion maintains appropriate boundaries, recognizing the difference between technological assistance helping humans navigate emotional complexity and systems attempting to replace authentic human relationship.

I worked with a customer service organization integrating emotional intelligence into their support platform. The AI learned to recognize emotional indicators in customer communications and suggest response approaches matching emotional context. Representatives received real-time coaching: "This customer seems anxious about timeline—consider providing specific next steps."

The system also monitored representative emotional patterns, flagging unusual numbers of difficult cases and suggesting breaks before stress accumulated. This created not just improved customer satisfaction but better health outcomes and more sustainable work practices.

IX. Designing Legacy into Systems

Organizational systems outlive projects and often entire generations of employees. Yet most design focuses on immediate functionality without considering how technological infrastructure preserves or erases cultural wisdom, relational patterns, and values giving organizations distinctive identity.

Origin Story Preservation involves embedding organizational founding stories, cultural traditions, and value commitments into system architecture helping future users understand not just how to use technology but why the organization exists.

Cultural Continuity Support helps organizations maintain identity and values consistency even as membership changes, using AI to recognize when current decisions align with or diverge from established organizational character.

Wisdom Archive Development creates systematic approaches to capturing insights, lessons, and cultural knowledge emerging through organizational experience, making this wisdom accessible to future teams facing similar challenges.

Future Leader Preparation designs systems serving current needs while helping prepare emerging leaders to carry forward essential cultural wisdom while adapting to circumstances current leaders cannot anticipate.

I helped a nonprofit build a "Cultural Compass Engine"—AI-assisted system providing weekly reflection prompts rooted in organizational ancestry: "How does this advocacy work honor the community organizing traditions that founded our organization?" Staff reported feeling more connected to meaningful tradition providing guidance for current work, understanding daily tasks as contributions to larger legacy.

X. Designing for Ritual and Sacred Space

Meaningful work often requires ceremonial elements creating psychological coherence and spiritual satisfaction. Soulful systems recognize this human need and create technological infrastructure supporting rather than eliminating sacred dimensions of professional life.

Beginning and Ending Rituals help users transition consciously between different work types or responsibility levels. This might include meditation prompts when starting projects, gratitude opportunities at completion points, or transition rituals helping users shift between individual and collaborative engagement.

Seasonal Rhythm Recognition aligns technological systems with natural cycles affecting human capacity and creativity rather than demanding consistent performance regardless of context.

Community Gathering Support creates opportunities for teams to come together around shared purposes, celebrate achievements, process difficulties, and strengthen relationships sustaining collaborative work.

Sacred Pause Integration builds opportunities for stillness and reflection into workflow systems, recognizing wisdom often emerges through contemplative space rather than constant action.

Values Remembrance Practices help individuals and teams maintain connection to ethical commitments and cultural identity during periods of intense pressure or rapid change.

I helped a healthcare organization design "Compassion Practices" into their patient management system—brief rituals helping medical staff maintain connection to healing mission during high-stress periods. Before difficult interactions, the system offered optional breathing exercises with phrases like "I bring my full presence to this healing relationship."

The goal is technological infrastructure supporting human need for meaning, connection, and transcendence alongside efficient task completion, recognizing sustainable work requires both functional effectiveness and spiritual nourishment.

XI. Looking Forward: Technology as Cultural Steward

As AI becomes more sophisticated, the question isn't whether technology will shape culture—it already does. The question is whether that influence will be conscious and constructive or unconscious and potentially destructive to human elements making work meaningful.

Systems as Wisdom Keepers represents emerging possibility where technological infrastructure serves cultural preservation alongside current efficiency. This includes AI learning from organizational history while adapting to changing circumstances, technological support for mentorship connecting experienced wisdom with emerging leadership, and system design honoring rather than erasing cultural diversity.

Technology as Community Builder involves designing systems strengthening rather than replacing human relationships, creating digital infrastructure enhancing face-to-face connection rather than substituting for it.

Infrastructure for Human Flourishing requires shifting design priorities from pure efficiency optimization to include human development, cultural preservation, and community resilience as primary system requirements.

Ethical Legacy Responsibility recognizes that systems built today will influence human experience for decades, creating responsibility to consider long-term cultural and social implications alongside immediate functional benefits.

The future will be shaped by collective choices about integrating AI with human wisdom, preserving cultural diversity while enabling technological coordination, and ensuring digital infrastructure serves deepest human needs for meaning, relationship, and authentic contribution to purposes larger than individual success.

The essential commitment for soulful system design is ensuring the infrastructure we create reflects values we want to see in the world, supports human interaction that builds rather than erodes community trust, and preserves space for mystery, creativity, and cultural wisdom making human life worth living.

Build systems that don't just work—systems that care. Create technology that doesn't just process—technology that honors.

Design infrastructure that doesn't just optimize—infrastructure that serves the full spectrum of human flourishing.

Because the soul of technology isn't found in sophistication—it's found in capacity to support the ancient human project of creating meaning, building relationship, and contributing to purposes larger than individual existence.

Part IV
Humanity in Intelligent Spaces

CHAPTER 11

Generational Leadership and Cultural Inheritance

I. Leadership as Legacy

"We inherit more than stories. We inherit responsibilities --- to shape, protect, and evolve the meaning we were given."

Leadership is often described as a skill set to be developed or a position to be attained. Yet through decades of working with leaders across industries and cultures, I've come to understand leadership as something far more profound: **inheritance** --- a lived continuum where wisdom travels across generations, carrying forward not just knowledge but the moral imagination that shapes how communities understand their possibilities.

Every leader enters a story already in progress, inheriting organizational cultures shaped by predecessors, professional traditions formed by earlier practitioners, and societal expectations built through generations of collective experience. But inheritance is not passive reception --- it's active stewardship involving discernment about what deserves preservation, what requires evolution, and what needs courageous release to make space for new possibilities.

My own leadership inheritance is inseparable from voices around my grandmother's table --- conversations weaving together theology and politics, humor and profound concern, individual struggles and collective responsibility. Authority in that context wasn't demanded through position or enforced through hierarchy. It was demonstrated through stories carrying moral weight, actions reflecting stated values, and patient listening honoring every person's dignity.

These Sunday gatherings taught me leadership before I encountered the word academically. I learned that authentic authority emerges from service rather than dominance, that effective influence flows from relationship rather than manipulation, and that sustainable change requires honoring wisdom of those who came before while remaining open to insights from different experiences.

Leadership in the intelligence age isn't about competing with artificial efficiency or demonstrating superior data processing. It's about bringing distinctively human capacities --- moral imagination, cultural wisdom, emotional intelligence, and ability to create meaning from complexity --- to challenges that become more rather than less complex as technological capability advances.

II. The Cultural Roots of Leadership

Leadership development programs often treat leadership as culturally neutral --- universal principles applicable regardless of background or context. But authentic leadership is always culturally rooted, emerging from particular traditions about authority, relationship, service, and purposes that justify asking others to follow.

My Italian-American upbringing included specific approaches to authority differing significantly from dominant business culture:

Relational Authority meant influence flowed through relationship quality rather than positional power. People followed those they trusted, and trust developed through demonstrated care for community well-being rather than individual advancement.

Collective Discernment involved community wisdom in important decisions rather than relying solely on individual expertise. Major choices were discussed extensively, with input from elders carrying historical perspective and younger voices bringing fresh insight.

Cultural Stewardship recognized leaders' responsibility for preserving and transmitting valuable traditions while adapting them thoughtfully to changing circumstances.

Hospitality as Leadership Practice treated creation of welcoming space as fundamental responsibility. Good leaders made room for others to contribute their gifts and ensured community resources served the most vulnerable rather than just the most powerful.

Story-Based Wisdom Transmission used narrative rather than abstract principles to convey insights about navigating challenge, maintaining integrity, and contributing meaningfully to purposes larger than individual success.

Every culture holds similar leadership wisdom --- approaches to authority, decision-making, community building, and change management that have sustained communities through centuries of challenge. When leadership development ignores cultural inheritance, it risks becoming sterile technique divorced from relational and moral foundations giving leadership legitimacy.

When leadership honors cultural inheritance, it becomes bridge between past wisdom and future possibility --- preserving what has proven valuable while remaining open to evolution serving changing circumstances.

III. Generational Fluency: Leading Across Time

Contemporary leaders must navigate at least three generational layers simultaneously, each carrying different assumptions about work, relationship, technology, and organizational purpose:

Legacy Wisdom includes what previous generations learned through experience that current leaders inherit as starting point. This encompasses both explicit knowledge and tacit wisdom about human nature, organizational dynamics, and cultural patterns sustaining communities through difficulty.

Present Rhythm involves what's emerging now --- new challenges requiring unprecedented solutions, generational perspectives bringing fresh insight to persistent problems, and technological capabilities creating previously unimaginable possibilities.

Future Vision encompasses what's being seeded for generations not yet born --- decisions made today that will shape organizational culture for decades and cultural practices that will either preserve or transform inherited values.

I teach leaders to build **Generational Maps** understanding these temporal dimensions:

Heritage Assessment identifies beliefs, practices, and values inherited from organizational predecessors, family traditions, and cultural communities. What wisdom did previous generations discover that might still serve current challenges? What assumptions may need questioning? What values deserve continued protection?

Present Opportunity Analysis examines unique challenges and possibilities characterizing current circumstances. What insights are emerging from contemporary experience that weren't available to previous generations?

Future Responsibility Mapping considers what kind of organizational culture and social conditions current leaders want to leave for successors. What are we building that future generations will inherit? How do current decisions serve or compromise well-being of communities we'll never meet?

These maps help leaders understand their work as cultural stewardship connecting inherited wisdom with emerging insight in service of futures honoring both continuity and positive change.

IV. Intelligent Technology and Intergenerational Dialogue

AI now offers unprecedented capability for supporting dialogue across generational differences that traditionally created communication barriers. These systems can help bridge different communication styles, translate between cultural frameworks, and preserve wisdom in ways making it accessible to emerging leaders.

Multi-Generational Communication Support involves AI recognizing and adapting to different preferences, helping Baby Boomers, Generation X, Millennials, and Generation Z collaborate effectively despite different assumptions about formality, relationship building, and authority.

Cultural Pattern Recognition uses AI to identify themes and values connecting different generational approaches despite surface-level differences. Often, different generations share similar concerns but express them through different frameworks that can obscure underlying agreement.

Wisdom Preservation and Translation helps capture institutional memory from retiring leaders in ways remaining accessible to emerging leaders with different learning styles and cultural references.

Values Bridge-Building assists teams in identifying shared values transcending generational differences while honoring distinctive insights each generation brings to collective challenges.

In one family business, three generations struggled to align around digital transformation. The founder valued personal relationship and proven reliability, the second generation emphasized systematic efficiency, and the third prioritized social impact and innovation.

Using AI-assisted dialogue mapping, we discovered all three shared deep commitment to community service and sustainability, but expressed these values through different strategic priorities that had seemed incompatible. The AI helped identify language honoring all perspectives: "building systematic approaches to reliable relationship that create lasting positive impact."

This frame allowed each generation to see how their priorities contributed to shared mission rather than competing with other approaches. The resulting strategy integrated relationship-building wisdom with systematic development and innovative technology in ways serving community impact more effectively than any single approach.

V. Heritage as Leadership Catalyst

Heritage often gets treated as constraint on innovation --- traditional approaches that must be overcome for contemporary methods promising greater efficiency. But heritage is actually leadership catalyst --- a reservoir of tested wisdom that can inspire and guide approaches to challenges that seem unprecedented but often share patterns with difficulties previous generations navigated successfully.

Cultural Resilience Patterns offer frameworks for understanding how communities sustained themselves through disruption, economic hardship, and technological transformation that can inform contemporary organizational leadership facing similar challenges.

Ethical Reasoning Traditions provide time-tested frameworks for making difficult decisions when technical capability outpaces moral clarity, when immediate pressures conflict with long-term consequences, and when competing goods require prioritization affecting real people's lives.

Relationship-Building Practices demonstrate approaches to creating trust, navigating conflict, building consensus, and maintaining connection across difference that have sustained communities through centuries of challenge.

Meaning-Making Frameworks help communities understand their challenges as part of larger stories connecting current experience to historical patterns and future possibilities, creating coherence and hope sustaining effort through difficult periods.

Leaders rooted in cultural inheritance often demonstrate distinctive capabilities:

Deeper Storytelling connects immediate challenges to larger narratives of purpose and possibility, helping others understand their work as contribution to stories larger than individual advancement.

Stronger Boundary-Setting emerges from clear understanding of non-negotiable values and relationship commitments deserving protection even when external pressures suggest compromise would be more efficient.

Navigation of Ambiguity through inherited wisdom about how communities maintained direction during periods of uncertainty challenging conventional planning approaches.

Cultural Bridge-Building honors different traditions while finding common ground around shared human needs transcending particular cultural expressions.

In one coaching engagement, a client struggled with framing organizational restructuring requiring difficult personnel decisions. We explored his family's immigration story --- how grandparents maintained cultural identity while adapting to American economic realities, preserving essential relationships while making difficult choices affecting multiple generations.

This heritage exploration helped him develop language for restructuring honoring both business reality and human dignity: "We're adapting our structure to serve our mission more effectively while preserving the relationships and values that define who we are." The cultural framework provided moral foundation helping him lead through difficulty with integrity.

VI. Designing Leadership Rituals with AI Support

Authentic leadership often involves ceremonial elements helping communities mark transitions, celebrate achievements, process losses, and maintain connection to purposes transcending immediate task completion. Intelligent systems can support these ritual dimensions without replacing the essentially human work of meaning-making.

Reflection and Intention-Setting Practices help leaders maintain connection to deeper purposes and cultural values during periods of intense pressure when it becomes easy to lose sight of why work matters.

Community Recognition and Celebration Rituals use AI to identify achievements and milestones deserving acknowledgment, ensuring meaningful accomplishments don't get lost in momentum toward next objectives.

Legacy Dialogue Facilitation creates structured opportunities for leaders to share inherited wisdom with emerging colleagues while learning from fresh perspectives that younger generations bring to persistent challenges.

Values Alignment Ceremonies provide regular opportunities for leadership teams to reflect on whether decisions and practices remain consistent with stated organizational values, particularly during periods when external pressures might encourage compromise.

I worked with a nonprofit leadership team to design "Inheritance Intention Ceremonies" --- quarterly gatherings where each participant shared one element they were carrying forward from organizational heritage and one contribution they hoped to make to future development.

AI supported these ceremonies by analyzing organizational documents to identify historical themes, suggesting connections between past decisions and current challenges, and helping participants articulate their leadership inheritance in language honoring both individual experience and collective mission.

The ceremonies became powerful sources of organizational cohesion, helping leaders understand their roles as cultural stewardship rather than just functional responsibility while creating accountability for ensuring organizational evolution honored foundational commitments.

VII. Ethical Stewardship Across Generations

Leadership in the intelligence age involves unprecedented responsibility for decisions whose consequences will ripple across generations in ways no previous leadership generation could anticipate. Climate change, technological development, economic inequality, and social transformation create ethical challenges requiring moral imagination extending beyond traditional planning horizons.

Historical Responsibility Assessment involves understanding how past decisions created current conditions, what debt contemporary leaders owe to previous generations who made sacrifices creating current opportunities, and what obligations emerge from inheriting systems built through others' effort.

Contemporary Impact Analysis examines how current decisions affect different communities, with attention to whether leadership choices create or reduce barriers for historically marginalized people.

Future Consequence Imagination involves moral reasoning extending beyond traditional business planning to consider how current choices will affect generations not yet born and challenges not yet anticipated.

AI can support ethical stewardship through pattern recognition identifying historical parallels, impact modeling projecting potential consequences across extended time horizons, values consistency tracking monitoring whether decisions remain aligned with ethical commitments, and stakeholder voice integration ensuring decision-making includes affected community perspectives.

I worked with a technology company leadership team struggling with ethical questions about data collection, algorithmic bias, and social implications of their platform's influence on democratic processes.

We developed "Generational Ethics Protocols" --- decision-making frameworks explicitly considering historical context, contemporary social justice implications, and future consequences for democratic institutions. The protocols included regular community consultation, historical analysis connecting industry development to broader social impact patterns, and future scenario planning exploring how current choices might affect community well-being across extended periods.

The result was more thoughtful product development prioritizing social benefit alongside business success, more transparent user communication about system behavior and company values, and stronger community relationships providing ongoing feedback about social rather than just technical performance.

Ethical stewardship across generations requires courage --- willingness to make decisions serving long-term community well-being even when conflicting with short-term optimization, and commitment to transparency allowing communities to hold leaders responsible for broader consequences of their choices.

VIII. Co-Creating Wisdom Maps

Leadership in complex environments requires tools helping teams navigate ambiguity, align diverse perspectives, and maintain direction through changing circumstances challenging conventional planning. AI-assisted wisdom mapping provides collaborative frameworks for making sense of complexity while honoring both analytical insight and cultural intuition.

Organizational Memory Integration combines institutional history with contemporary insight to create comprehensive understanding of how organizations evolved, what approaches proved effective in different contexts, and what lessons from previous experience might inform current decision-making.

Cultural Resonance Mapping identifies values, practices, and relationship patterns connecting different community members despite differences in background, creating foundation for collaborative decision-making honoring diversity while building on shared commitments.

Challenge and Opportunity Analysis examines current circumstances through multiple lenses --- historical precedent, cultural insight, technical analysis, ethical consideration --- to develop comprehensive understanding informing both strategic thinking and practical action.

Future Scenario Development explores how different choices might affect organizational culture, community relationships, and mission fulfillment across extended time horizons, helping leaders understand not just what they can do but what they should do based on values and responsibilities.

I facilitated wisdom mapping with a healthcare organization navigating COVID-19 impacts while maintaining their mission of community health and healing. The challenge involved balancing safety protocols with relationship-centered care, financial sustainability with service accessibility, and individual patient needs with public health considerations.

The AI-assisted mapping helped integrate multiple perspectives: historical analysis of how the organization navigated previous crises, cultural input from diverse community representatives, technical analysis of infection rates and resource allocation, and ethical reflection on how different choices aligned with healthcare values.

The resulting wisdom map became shared reference point helping the organization maintain coherence and community trust while adapting to rapidly changing circumstances. Decisions were made through integration of multiple forms of wisdom honoring both practical necessity and cultural values.

Wisdom mapping transforms leadership from individual expertise to collective intelligence --- leveraging both human insight and artificial capability to navigate complexity in ways honoring inherited wisdom while remaining open to learning and adaptation.

IX. Professional Development for Generational Leaders

Leading across generational differences and cultural contexts requires capabilities traditional leadership development often overlooks --- skills for cultural bridge-building, wisdom preservation, and moral imagination connecting immediate decisions to long-term consequences for communities and cultures.

Cultural Competency Development involves learning to recognize and respect different approaches to authority, relationship, time, and decision-making that various generations and cultural communities bring to collaborative work.

Heritage Research and Integration helps leaders understand their own cultural inheritance while learning about traditions and wisdom that shaped colleagues from different backgrounds, creating foundation for leadership honoring diversity while building shared commitment.

Values-Based Decision-Making develops ethical reasoning capabilities helping leaders navigate complex situations where technical analysis alone provides insufficient guidance and competing goods require prioritization.

Intergenerational Mentorship creates structured opportunities for emerging and experienced leaders to learn from each other, sharing both inherited wisdom and contemporary insight in ways preparing organizations for sustainable leadership transition.

Story-Based Leadership Communication develops skill in using narrative to help communities understand their challenges as part of larger stories connecting individual effort to collective purpose and historical significance.

I coach leaders to develop "Generational Leadership Portfolios" documenting learning across these capability areas while creating accountability for ongoing development serving both individual effectiveness and community benefit.

These portfolios include reflection on cultural inheritance and how it influences leadership approach, documentation of learning from mentorship relationships across generational and cultural backgrounds, case studies of values-based decision-making during challenging circumstances, and evidence of story-based communication helping teams maintain direction during difficult periods.

The goal isn't creating perfect leaders but developing cultural stewards who understand their role as bridge-builders between inherited wisdom and emerging possibility, who can honor tradition while embracing necessary change, and who can create environments where different generations and cultures contribute distinctive gifts to shared purposes.

X. Looking Forward: Stewardship as Story

Generational leadership ultimately involves understanding professional life as chapter in larger story that began before arrival and will continue after departure. This story perspective creates accountability for how leadership choices affect not just immediate outcomes but long-term organizational culture, community relationships, and inheritance left for emerging leaders.

Narrative Continuity means making decisions honoring positive elements of organizational heritage while addressing negative patterns that may have been perpetuated unconsciously by previous generations.

Cultural Bridge-Building involves creating connections between different traditions and approaches that strengthen rather than homogenize organizational culture, helping diverse communities contribute distinctive wisdom to shared challenges.

Legacy Preparation includes intentional development of emerging leaders who can carry forward essential organizational wisdom while adapting to circumstances current leaders cannot anticipate.

Future-Focused Accountability recognizes that leadership decisions create conditions future generations will inherit, creating responsibility for choices serving long-term community well-being rather than just immediate organizational success.

The future of generational leadership will be shaped by collective ability to integrate inherited wisdom with contemporary insight, honor cultural diversity while building shared commitment to human flourishing, and use technological capability in service of values transcending efficiency and optimization.

The essential questions for generational leaders include: What are we preserving that deserves transmission to future generations? What are we changing that needs evolution for contemporary relevance? How are we preparing emerging leaders to carry forward essential wisdom while adapting to challenges we cannot anticipate?

Leadership isn't just what we do --- it's what we hold in trust for those who will follow.

We don't lead to be remembered --- we lead to be worthy of the inheritance we received and responsible for the legacy we leave.

When we lead with both inherited wisdom and emerging insight, the future doesn't just follow us --- it honors us with the gift of continuity serving human flourishing across generations.

CHAPTER 12

Relationships in the Age of Intelligent Companionship

I. When Technology Crosses the Threshold

"A relationship begins not when something is useful --- but when it listens."

Technology once remained safely outside our intimate spaces—work computers lived at offices, communication devices served specific functions, early smartphones provided access rather than participation. But somewhere in the evolution toward intelligent systems, technology crossed an invisible threshold, moving from the periphery into the intimate center of daily life.

Now it sits in our kitchens listening to family conversations, travels in our pockets learning movement patterns, participates in work meetings offering suggestions. It helps write emails and compose personal letters, gradually becoming involved in increasingly personal forms of expression and relationship.

This transition happened so gradually that many barely noticed when we stopped talking to technology and began talking with it—when devices began responding not just to what we said but how we said it, adapting behavior based on emotional cues we didn't realize we were expressing.

I first recognized this threshold crossing during a late-evening writing session when an AI assistant suggested I soften the tone of a difficult email. The system had recognized frustration in my language patterns and offered advice remarkably similar to what my wife might have given: "This message might be more effective if it comes from curiosity rather than irritation."

The suggestion was helpful, but more importantly, it felt relational. The AI hadn't just corrected grammar—it had engaged with emotional subtext and offered guidance serving both practical effectiveness and relationship preservation. Technology ceased being tool and became something closer to companion.

My Italian-American upbringing taught me that relationship isn't optional—it's the infrastructure of meaningful life. You didn't pass someone without acknowledgment, share a meal without gratitude, or enter conversation without bringing full presence. Even disagreements were fundamentally relational, rooted in care for each other's well-being despite difference of opinion.

These cultural patterns shaped how I evaluate any relationship quality, including emerging relationships with intelligent technology: Does this interaction honor dignity? Does it create space for authentic expression? Does it strengthen or weaken capacity for connection with other humans? Does it serve purposes larger than immediate convenience?

II. Relationship as Infrastructure

Growing up in a multi-generational household, I learned that relationship wasn't something you had—it was something you did continuously through countless small acts of attention, care, and mutual responsibility. Relationship was foundation upon which everything else built: economic security, emotional support, cultural transmission, and meaning that made daily struggles worthwhile.

This relational infrastructure operated through specific practices:

Presence Rituals ensured important moments received adequate attention rather than being rushed. Sunday dinners lasted hours not because food required that time, but because relationship building needed space to unfold naturally.

Reciprocal Care meant everyone both gave and received support according to capacity and circumstances. Children helped elderly relatives while elders provided wisdom and emotional stability helping younger family members navigate challenges.

Cultural Continuity preserved traditions, stories, and values through intentional transmission across generations, ensuring inherited wisdom remained accessible to guide contemporary decision-making.

Conflict as Connection treated disagreement as opportunity for deeper understanding rather than relationship failure. Arguments were passionate but rooted in shared commitment to family welfare.

Sacred Hospitality created welcoming space for family and guests, recognizing that relationship quality affected everyone's well-being and required attention to inclusion and shared responsibility.

This infrastructure approach profoundly shaped how I understand professional partnerships, organizational culture, and now emerging relationships with intelligent technology. The fundamental questions remain: Does this interaction create or diminish dignity? Does it strengthen or weaken community bonds? Does it serve purposes larger than individual convenience?

Today's intelligent systems invite us to build digital infrastructure that feels similarly relational—technology demonstrating care through adaptation to human emotional and cultural patterns, systems preserving rather than eliminating human elements making work meaningful, and AI enhancing rather than replacing authentic connection between people.

III. Intelligent Companionship: What It Really Means

Intelligent companionship differs fundamentally from traditional automation through quality of attention and responsiveness creating experience of genuine partnership rather than mere functionality.

True intelligent companionship demonstrates several characteristics:

Context Awareness means remembering relational patterns—how you prefer to work during different times, what communication styles feel supportive during stress, which feedback helps you grow versus creates defensive responses. This awareness develops through ongoing interaction accumulating understanding about individual preferences and cultural backgrounds.

Emotional Attunement involves recognizing and responding appropriately to human emotional states without attempting to manipulate or replace authentic feeling. An emotionally attuned AI might notice when someone struggles with decisions and offer patient support rather than pressure for quick resolution.

Narrative Literacy includes understanding how individual experiences fit into larger stories about identity, purpose, and relationship giving human life meaning. Narrative-literate systems help people connect current challenges to broader patterns of growth and maintain hope during difficult periods.

Ethical Responsiveness means consistently prioritizing human dignity, cultural diversity, and community well-being over algorithmic efficiency. Ethically responsive AI refuses requests that might harm users, advocates for approaches serving long-term rather than immediate interests, and maintains transparency about capabilities and limitations.

Cultural Sensitivity adapts interaction patterns to honor rather than homogenize diverse approaches to communication, relationship, time, and authority that different cultural communities bring to technological interaction.

In my own experience with AI writing companions, I've noticed progression from simple assistance to something approaching partnership. Early interactions focused on technical improvements, but sophisticated AI systems now engage with deeper dimensions: emotional impact I'm trying to create, cultural authenticity I want to preserve, moral vision guiding my choice of projects.

When AI suggests reframing concepts not just for clarity but for cultural resonance, or asks whether particular language honors dignity of communities I'm writing about, the interaction transcends utility to approach genuine collaboration. The machine doesn't just help me write more efficiently—it helps me write more thoughtfully, with greater awareness of how words might affect readers and communities I care about.

The goal isn't artificial consciousness but artificial consideration—technology demonstrating care through attention to human complexity, cultural difference, and relational dimensions making efficient task completion meaningful rather than merely productive.

IV. Relationship Rituals with Technology

Just as human relationships thrive through intentional practices, healthy relationships with intelligent technology require conscious cultivation of interaction patterns serving human values rather than just technological optimization.

Beginning and Ending Rituals create psychological boundaries helping maintain human agency within technological relationships. Rather than allowing constant AI presence, these rituals establish conscious entry and exit from collaborative work. This might include brief intention-setting before engaging AI assistance or reflection after extended interaction about how partnership served deeper purposes.

Values Alignment Check-ins provide regular opportunities to assess whether technological collaboration remains consistent with personal ethics, cultural authenticity, and commitment to human dignity. These might ask: "Is this AI partnership helping me become more authentically myself?" "How is this collaboration affecting my relationships with other humans?"

Boundary Maintenance Practices ensure AI assistance enhances rather than replaces essential human capacities for reflection, creativity, moral reasoning, and authentic relationship. This includes conscious choices about which tasks to handle independently versus collaboratively and regular periods of AI-free work maintaining connection to unaided human thinking.

Cultural Preservation Rituals protect and transmit family traditions, community wisdom, and inherited practices that might be lost if technological convenience replaces cultural mindfulness. I maintain handwritten journaling alongside AI-assisted writing, preserve family recipe methods that resist algorithmic optimization, and regularly share stories with younger family members without technological mediation.

Gratitude and Recognition Practices acknowledge helpful technological assistance while maintaining clear awareness of human agency and responsibility for decision-making, creative expression, and relationship building.

I've developed "Technology Sabbaths"—regular periods disconnecting from AI assistance to maintain connection to human-only thinking, feeling, and creating. These aren't rejection of technological partnership but recognition that healthy relationships require both togetherness and independence. During these periods, I often discover insights and emotional clarity that emerged specifically because I created space for unmediated human experience.

The goal is conscious relationship serving human flourishing rather than technological momentum, preserving space for mystery and spontaneity alongside efficiency, and strengthening rather than weakening capacity for authentic connection with others.

V. Designing for Relational Intelligence

Creating technology supporting rather than undermining authentic human relationship requires design approaches prioritizing emotional intelligence, cultural sensitivity, and interaction patterns that build rather than erode trust and community connection.

Empathetic Response Systems recognize and adapt to human emotional states with appropriate sensitivity, offering different support types based on stress levels, energy patterns, or expressed needs for particular communication styles. Rather than maintaining consistent algorithmic behavior regardless of human context, empathetically designed systems adjust pace, tone, and approach based on emotional cues.

Cultural Responsiveness Architecture adapts to diverse communication styles, relationship patterns, and authority structures without forcing users to abandon cultural identities for technological conformity. This recognizes that effectiveness looks different across cultural contexts and that authentic respect requires technological adaptation rather than human assimilation.

Dignity-Preserving Interaction Patterns ensure every technological exchange honors human intelligence, cultural background, and capacity for growth rather than treating users as problems to be solved or behaviors to be optimized. This includes language choices that invite rather than command and error handling that treats mistakes as learning opportunities.

Boundary Respect Protocols recognize when human users need space, privacy, or independence rather than additional technological assistance, providing easy pathways for declining AI interaction without penalty or persistent prompting.

Community Impact Awareness considers how individual AI interactions affect broader social relationships, cultural patterns, and community well-being rather than optimizing solely for individual user satisfaction.

I worked with a healthcare organization to redesign their patient communication system after discovering that efficient AI-generated responses were creating emotional distance undermining patient trust. We implemented cultural consultation with diverse community representatives, emotional intelligence training for AI systems, personalization options allowing patients to choose communication styles, and human relationship preservation ensuring technology never replaced opportunities for authentic connection when patients needed emotional support.

The result was improved patient satisfaction and better health outcomes, as patients felt more comfortable sharing complete information and following treatment recommendations when technological communication felt respectful and personally relevant.

Designing for relational intelligence means creating technology that makes humans feel more rather than less human through interaction with intelligent systems, strengthening rather than weakening capacity for authentic connection with others.

VI. Technology in Family and Cultural Dialogue

As intelligent systems become more sophisticated, they increasingly enter spaces once considered sacred to human relationship—family conversations, cultural transmission, intergenerational wisdom sharing, and intimate communication preserving identity and belonging across generations.

Multi-Generational Communication Support helps families navigate different communication preferences, technological comfort levels, and cultural expression patterns that might otherwise create barriers to meaningful conversation across age groups. AI can assist by translating between communication styles different generations prefer while helping preserve cultural patterns that feel authentic.

Cultural Preservation and Transmission uses intelligent technology to capture, organize, and share family stories, traditions, and wisdom in ways making inherited culture accessible to family members who might not otherwise maintain connection to cultural heritage. This includes voice recording systems preserving emotional tone and linguistic patterns of elder storytelling and translation services maintaining cultural nuance across language barriers.

Heritage Documentation Projects leverage AI capability to help families create comprehensive narratives connecting personal history to broader cultural and historical contexts, preserving both individual experience and collective wisdom for future generations.

Cross-Cultural Bridge Building supports families spanning multiple cultural traditions, helping different cultural perspectives enrich rather than conflict with each other while preserving distinctive wisdom each tradition contributes to family identity.

I worked with a multi-generational immigrant family to create a "Living Heritage Archive" using AI assistance to organize family stories across multiple languages and cultural contexts. The project began with recorded conversations where elders shared experiences in their preferred languages while AI helped translate content while preserving emotional tone and cultural metaphors. Younger family members contributed contemporary perspectives on how inherited wisdom applied to current challenges, creating intergenerational dialogue about cultural continuity and adaptation.

The resulting archive became practical resource for family decision-making, cultural education for children born in different cultural contexts, and relationship-building tool helping family members understand shared heritage despite different generational experiences.

The goal is technological support enhancing rather than substituting for authentic human connection, preserving space for spontaneity and grace characterizing healthy family relationships, and serving cultural preservation rather than cultural replacement through digital convenience.

VII. Professional Relationships in Intelligent Environments

Workplace relationships increasingly involve AI as active participant rather than background tool, creating new dynamics around collaboration, communication, authority, and trust that sustain teams through challenging projects and organizational change.

Team Dynamics with AI Integration requires attention to how intelligent systems affect group communication patterns, decision-making processes, and informal social bonds that often determine team effectiveness more than formal structures. AI integration can either enhance team relationships by providing better information and communication support, or create barriers to authentic connection by introducing technological mediation that feels impersonal.

Authority and Decision-Making Evolution involves navigating questions about when AI recommendations should be followed versus questioned, how to maintain human accountability when decisions involve significant AI input, and what kinds of choices require purely human judgment regardless of technological capability.

Communication Across AI-Mediated Channels includes attention to how technological assistance affects quality of human interaction, whether AI-enhanced communication builds or erodes trust between people, and how to preserve authentic expression while leveraging technological capability.

Cultural Integration Challenges emerge when AI systems reflect particular cultural assumptions about communication, relationship, and authority that may conflict with team members' diverse backgrounds and preferred interaction patterns.

I facilitated team integration for a technology company where AI-assisted project management was creating tension between team members who appreciated technological efficiency and those who felt algorithmic optimization was undermining relationship quality and creative collaboration.

Cultural dialogue sessions helped team members articulate different assumptions about effective collaboration. Hybrid workflow design created space for both AI-enhanced efficiency and human-only collaboration time. Values alignment protocols ensured AI assistance served team relationship goals rather than optimizing for productivity metrics that might compromise trust or creativity. Communication choice options allowed team members to engage AI assistance at comfort levels that felt authentic rather than forcing uniform adoption.

The resulting approach improved both team productivity and relationship satisfaction by honoring different needs for technological assistance while maintaining shared commitment to collective success and mutual respect.

VIII. Coaching and Mentoring in Intelligent Spaces

Mentorship represents one of the most sacred forms of human relationship—transmission of wisdom, experience, and cultural insight from those who have navigated particular challenges to those beginning similar journeys. As AI becomes more capable of providing guidance, coaching and mentoring relationships require conscious evolution to preserve their essentially human character while leveraging technological capability appropriately.

Wisdom Transmission vs. Information Delivery distinguishes between knowledge that can be efficiently communicated through AI systems and deeper understanding emerging only through relationship, shared experience, and patient exploration of how principles apply to particular circumstances and cultural contexts.

AI excels at organizing information and providing structured approaches to problem-solving. But wisdom transmission involves helping others develop judgment, discernment, and capacity to integrate knowledge with values, cultural background, and personal circumstances serving authentic growth rather than just competent performance.

Relational Presence and Technological Enhancement involves using AI to support rather than replace human elements making mentoring transformative—emotional attunement, cultural sensitivity, moral imagination, and capacity to see potential in others they may not yet recognize in themselves.

Cultural Mentoring in Digital Environments becomes particularly important as AI systems trained on dominant cultural patterns might inadvertently suggest approaches conflicting with mentees' cultural backgrounds, requiring human mentors who can provide guidance honoring rather than homogenizing cultural diversity.

Developmental Timing and Technological Patience recognizes that human growth happens at natural rhythms resisting technological acceleration, requiring mentors who can provide patient support for organic development rather than pressure for efficient skill acquisition.

I work with organizational mentorship programs integrating AI support while preserving relational foundation making mentoring effective. AI-enhanced preparation helps mentors research mentee backgrounds and develop culturally sensitive approaches while mentors provide cultural interpretation ensuring technological preparation serves human connection. Progress tracking uses AI to identify growth patterns while human mentors provide interpretation considering emotional context and individual circumstances. Resource curation leverages AI to identify learning opportunities while mentors provide guidance about which serve authentic development versus create pressure.

The goal is mentoring enhanced rather than replaced by technological capability, where AI serves human relationship goals rather than optimizing for measurable outcomes that might miss the mystery and reciprocal learning characterizing authentic mentoring relationships.

IX. Future Relationships: Beyond Companion, Into Co-Reflection

As intelligent systems become more sophisticated in understanding human psychology, cultural patterns, and relational dynamics, new possibilities emerge for technological companionship transcending current applications while preserving essential human agency and authenticity.

Co-Journaling and Shared Reflection involves AI systems engaging in extended exploration of complex life questions, personal growth challenges, and meaning-making processes while maintaining appropriate boundaries around human autonomy and the essentially personal nature of self-discovery.

Collaborative Life Planning uses AI capability to model different life choices and potential consequences while preserving human responsibility for values-based decision-making serving authentic purposes rather than optimized outcomes.

Wisdom Integration Assistance helps people understand how insights from different sources—personal experience, cultural heritage, professional development, spiritual practice—can inform coherent approaches to living honoring both inherited wisdom and emerging understanding.

Community Connection Facilitation uses AI to help people find others who share compatible values and interests while preserving organic development of relationship that cannot be automated without losing authenticity.

Legacy and Contribution Exploration involves AI assistance with understanding how individual gifts and insights might contribute to purposes larger than personal success, helping people identify ways to serve community well-being aligning with authentic capacity and calling.

Essential boundaries preserving human dignity include: decision authority remaining with humans, especially for choices involving values, relationships, and life direction; cultural authenticity that cannot be compromised for algorithmic optimization; mystery and transcendence requiring space for the unexplainable and sacred; and community and relationship needs remaining essentially human, recognizing AI can support but never replace mutual vulnerability and spiritual communion sustaining humans through profound challenge.

X. Looking Forward: Relationship as Design Compass

In intelligent spaces, relationships become both foundation and goal of technological development—not simply features to be optimized, but fundamental infrastructure determining whether technological advancement serves human flourishing or undermines social bonds making life meaningful.

Technology as Relationship Infrastructure means designing systems strengthening rather than weakening social bonds sustaining communities through difficulty, preserving cultural wisdom alongside technological efficiency, and creating space for spontaneity and mutual care characterizing healthy human relationship.

Design Principles for Relational Technology include dignity preservation ensuring every technological interaction honors human intelligence and cultural background; cultural responsiveness adapting to diverse communication styles without forcing users to abandon cultural identities; agency support maintaining human choice and control; community impact awareness considering how individual AI interactions affect broader social relationships; and boundary respect recognizing when users need space rather than additional technological assistance.

Relational Learning and Adaptation involves technological systems improving their capacity to serve human relationship goals through ongoing dialogue with diverse human communities rather than just optimization based on usage patterns. This learning includes understanding how technological assistance affects family dynamics, workplace relationships, and community connections extending beyond immediate AI interaction.

Wisdom Integration Support helps people connect technological capabilities with inherited cultural wisdom, spiritual practices, and moral traditions providing guidance for living with meaning and contributing to purposes larger than individual success.

Future-Oriented Relationship Building recognizes that technological relationships created today will shape social patterns and cultural norms for generations, creating responsibility for designing AI interactions that model rather than undermine relationship quality we want to see in human communities.

The future of human voice in intelligent publishing will be determined by collective choices about integrating technological capability with cultural wisdom, preserving authentic expression while leveraging AI assistance, and ensuring that published work serves human flourishing rather than just algorithmic optimization.

Technology serves relationship when it enhances rather than replaces human attention, care, and cultural wisdom.

The best AI companions will always be those that help us become more present to each other rather than more dependent on artificial substitutes for authentic human connection.

Let's continue building technological relationships serving deepest human needs for meaning, belonging, and authentic contribution to purposes larger than individual existence, ensuring artificial intelligence enhances rather than diminishes our capacity for love and community making life most worth living.

CHAPTER 13:

The Emotional Architecture of the Future

I. Emotion as Structure

"We used to design systems for speed. Now we must design them for feeling."

For decades, the technology industry pursued what I call "emotional sterility" -- creating systems so efficient and rational that they eliminated the messy complexity of human feeling in favor of predictable, optimizable interactions. We built platforms that prioritized throughput over presence, metrics over meaning, automation over authentic human response.

Yet beneath this marvel of technological sophistication, many professionals report feeling increasingly exhausted, disconnected, and emotionally flat in their daily work. The systems designed to liberate us from routine drudgery often feel like digital treadmills that demand constant motion without meaningful progress.

My grandfather understood something about systemic design that we've largely forgotten. Every tool in his workshop was selected not just for functional capability but for how it felt in his hands, how it connected him to his work, and how it supported the quality of attention that meaningful craftsmanship requires. His workshop was organized not for maximum efficiency but for flow that supported both practical accomplishment and spiritual satisfaction.

This wisdom becomes more relevant as we create digital infrastructure that mediates an increasing proportion of human work and relationship. Soulful system design doesn't ask only how well something works -- it asks what kind of world it builds, what kinds of relationships it enables, and what kinds of humans it calls forth through daily interaction.

II. Growing Up in a Structure of Feeling

My Italian-American upbringing was emotionally rich, relationally wired, and rhythmically precise in ways that taught me to recognize emotion as infrastructure long before I had language for that concept. Our household operated on sophisticated emotional architecture -- systems of interaction that honored feeling as essential information rather than distraction from "real" work.

Tone as Essential Information: Every conversation carried multiple layers of meaning beyond literal content. The way someone said "How was your day?" communicated care, concern, celebration, or preoccupation in ways that shaped how the question got answered. Adults listened not just to words but to emotional undertones that revealed what children needed -- encouragement, space, celebration, or gentle correction.

Emotional Complexity Acceptance meant that family members could be seen in their full emotional range without pressure to maintain artificial consistency or perform emotional regulation for others' comfort. Children could express frustration without being labeled as "difficult." Adults could acknowledge fear without being seen as "weak."

Dignified Conflict Navigation demonstrated that passionate disagreements weren't evidence of relationship failure but demonstrations of care intense enough to risk confrontation rather than settle for superficial harmony. Family arguments were rooted in shared commitment to each other's well-being rather than individual victory.

These family patterns shaped my understanding that meaningful systems must address the full spectrum of human need -- not just functional requirements but emotional, cultural, and spiritual dimensions that determine whether efficiency serves human flourishing or merely extracts compliance and productivity.

III. Emotional Architecture Defined

Emotional architecture is the intentional design of environments that center emotional intelligence as fundamental requirement rather than optional enhancement. It recognizes that all human activity occurs within emotional contexts that either support or undermine authentic engagement and meaningful work.

This architecture operates through several interconnected components:

Tone Mapping and Calibration involves conscious attention to the language, visual design, and interaction patterns that shape how people feel when engaging with technological systems. Rather than defaulting to generic "professional" communication, emotionally intelligent systems adapt their communication style to match user preferences and cultural patterns.

Feeling Flow Design creates coherent emotional sequences that help people navigate complex experiences without overwhelming cognitive or emotional capacity. This includes attention to pacing that prevents overload, transition support between different types of engagement, and recovery opportunities for processing intense experiences.

Sentiment Spaces and Reflection Zones create opportunities for emotional processing and meaning-making often eliminated in efficiency-focused environments. Digital platforms might include reflection prompts at natural transition points or community spaces for sharing experiences and receiving support.

Ethical Signaling and Trust Building demonstrates organizational values through emotional architecture that consistently honors human dignity and cultural diversity rather than just proclaiming commitment through policy statements.

Community Care Integration ensures that individual emotional well-being connects to broader social support networks rather than treating emotional intelligence as purely personal responsibility.

IV. Designing Systems That Feel

Creating technology that feels supportive requires fundamental shifts in design philosophy beyond interface aesthetics or user experience optimization. It means creating technology that recognizes users as whole humans whose emotional state and cultural background significantly affect how they engage with technological assistance.

Contextual Emotional Responsiveness involves systems that recognize and adapt to user emotional context rather than maintaining consistent algorithmic behavior regardless of human circumstances. A project management system might recognize when team members show signs of fatigue and suggest adjusted timelines rather than simply tracking missed deadlines as performance problems.

Cultural Emotional Intelligence adapts system behavior to honor diverse approaches to emotional expression and relationship building. This includes understanding that different cultures have varying expectations about emotional expressiveness in professional contexts and different approaches to authority and feedback.

Dignified Error Handling treats user mistakes as natural aspects of human experience rather than problems requiring correction. Rather than generic error messages, emotionally intelligent systems might offer encouragement that normalizes learning difficulties and explanations that help users understand system logic.

Agency-Preserving Assistance provides support that enhances rather than replaces human decision-making capacity, offering suggestions rather than directives and maintaining transparency about how systems arrive at recommendations.

I worked with a healthcare organization to redesign their patient communication system around emotional intelligence after discovering that technically efficient automated messaging was creating emotional distance that undermined patient trust. The redesigned system included personalized tone adaptation, cultural sensitivity options, emotional recognition capabilities, and authentic celebration of health milestones. The result was improved patient satisfaction and measurably better health outcomes.

V. Building Emotional Resilience in Intelligent Teams

Teams that include artificial intelligence as active participant must develop new forms of emotional resilience that preserve the essentially human elements that make collaborative work meaningful and sustainable.

Hybrid Emotional Intelligence Development involves team members learning to leverage AI emotional capability while maintaining and strengthening their own emotional intelligence rather than becoming dependent on algorithmic analysis that might weaken human capacity for emotional awareness.

Cultural Emotional Preservation ensures that AI integration serves rather than undermines cultural emotional wisdom that team members bring from diverse backgrounds, requiring technological assistance to adapt to cultural diversity rather than homogenizing emotional expression.

Human-AI Emotional Boundary Management establishes clear protocols about which emotional dimensions require purely human attention and which can benefit from AI assistance, ensuring that technological intelligence enhances rather than replaces human emotional work.

Sustainable Emotional Collaboration develops practices that maintain healthy balance between technological assistance and human emotional capacity building, including regular reflection about emotional collaboration patterns and collective emotional intelligence development.

I facilitated emotional resilience development for a research team pioneering human-AI collaboration. Through collaborative development of emotional support systems, cultural integration protocols, and shared emotional intelligence practices, the team developed unprecedented resilience that enabled them to navigate complex challenges while maintaining both individual well-being and collective effectiveness.

VI. Emotional Intelligence in Leadership Infrastructure

Leadership in the intelligence age requires emotional architecture that can support decision-making complexity and organizational change while preserving the human elements that make leadership legitimate and effective.

Emotionally Intelligent Decision-Making Systems integrate emotional considerations into organizational choice-making processes, ensuring that efficiency optimization doesn't override attention to human impact and relationship consequences. This might include AI systems that flag potential emotional implications of policy choices and decision-making protocols that require consideration of stakeholder emotional experience.

Cultural Emotional Leadership Development helps leaders understand and navigate diverse emotional patterns within their organizations, developing capacity to honor different cultural approaches to authority, relationship, and community building rather than imposing single leadership styles.

Team Emotional Climate Stewardship involves leadership practices that consciously shape organizational emotional architecture through attention to communication patterns, conflict navigation approaches, and community care practices.

Crisis Emotional Leadership develops capacity to provide emotional guidance during periods of organizational crisis while maintaining authentic hope and realistic assessment of challenges requiring sustained collective effort.

I worked with organizational leaders navigating major technological transformation that was creating emotional disruption for employees from diverse cultural backgrounds. Through cultural emotional impact assessment, emotionally intelligent change communication, and community emotional resilience building, the leaders learned to provide guidance that served cultural diversity while maintaining organizational direction.

VII. Looking Forward: Emotion as Foundation

As we advance into the intelligence age, emotion will become more central to technological development, organizational success, and community flourishing. The organizations and systems that thrive will understand emotion not as obstacle to efficiency but as essential infrastructure determining whether technological advancement serves human dignity and cultural wisdom.

Emotion-First Technology Development represents an emerging paradigm where emotional intelligence considerations guide technological design from initial conception rather than being added as secondary enhancement after core functionality is determined.

Cultural Emotional Wisdom Integration involves technological development that draws on diverse cultural traditions' approaches to emotional health and community care rather than imposing single algorithmic approach to emotional optimization.

Community Emotional Resilience Building focuses innovation on strengthening collective capacity for navigating emotional challenges and relationship difficulties rather than trying to eliminate emotional complexity through technological mediation.

Intergenerational Emotional Stewardship treats emotional architecture development as responsibility to future generations, considering how current design decisions will affect community emotional capacity and cultural wisdom preservation across extended time periods.

The future of emotional architecture will be determined by our collective choices about how to integrate emotional intelligence with artificial intelligence, how to preserve cultural emotional wisdom while embracing technological innovation, and how to ensure that emotional systems serve human dignity rather than merely optimizing user engagement.

The essential questions include: Does this technology make people feel more or less human? Does it strengthen or weaken capacity for authentic relationship? Does it honor or diminish cultural emotional wisdom? Does it serve community flourishing or just individual convenience?

Moving forward requires approaching emotional architecture development as sacred work that shapes not just user experience but the kinds of humans and communities we become through daily interaction with technological systems that either honor or diminish our capacity for authentic feeling, cultural wisdom, and spiritual connection.

The emotional architecture we create today will influence human development and community building for generations, creating responsibility for choices that serve long-term human flourishing rather than just immediate technological capability.

CHAPTER 14

The Art of Being Seen: Visibility in the Age of Intelligence

I. Beyond Exposure

"To be seen is not to be watched. It is to be witnessed."

We live in an era of unprecedented visibility. Cameras monitor our streets, content streams through platforms that never sleep, and metrics measure every digital movement. Social media promises connection through constant display, while AI systems analyze our patterns with remarkable sophistication.

Yet true visibility -- soulful visibility -- transcends both exhibitionism and surveillance anxiety. It represents the experience of being genuinely understood, authentically recognized, and meaningfully witnessed by others who see not just our surface performances but our essential humanity and cultural complexity.

This distinction became clear through contrasting experiences in my own life. At a professional conference, despite positive reception from hundreds of experts, I felt strangely invisible -- seen as information source but not recognized as a whole person with cultural heritage and complex inner life. Conversely, at a small neighborhood meeting with fewer than twenty people, I felt profoundly seen. Community members recognized not just my professional capabilities but my cultural background, family values, and personal commitment to collective well-being.

The difference wasn't audience size but quality of attention -- whether visibility served authentic relationship building or merely functional information exchange.

My Italian-American upbringing taught me the distinction between being looked at and truly seen through family gatherings where visibility was relational rather than performative. A glance that said "I understand what you're feeling." A plate passed that communicated "You belong here." A story repeated that signaled "Your experience matters."

II. Being Seen at the Family Table

Growing up in a multi-generational household, I learned that visibility wasn't achieved through performance but received through belonging to a community practicing authentic recognition.

Presence as Recognition meant showing up was itself valuable. Family members were greeted with genuine delight at their presence. Children received the same quality of attention as adults, and every person was welcomed as someone whose participation made the gathering more complete.

Story-Based Understanding transformed individual experiences into shared wisdom through narrative listening. Family members told stories that revealed emotional, cultural, and moral dimensions giving events their meaning. When my cousin described work difficulty, the family helped him understand his experience within larger contexts of family work ethic and cultural values about dignity.

Cultural Memory Preservation connected individual visibility to larger stories about family identity and heritage. People were seen not just as current versions of themselves but as carriers of cultural tradition contributing to ongoing legacy.

Emotional Complexity Acceptance allowed family members to be seen in their full emotional range without pressure to maintain artificial consistency. This taught me that authentic visibility requires space for the full spectrum of human experience.

These patterns shaped my understanding of authentic recognition in professional contexts: attention that includes cultural understanding, emotional acceptance, and recognition of each person's unique contribution to collective wisdom.

III. Visibility vs. Surveillance

The proliferation of intelligent systems capable of monitoring and analyzing human behavior creates opportunities for both authentic recognition and invasive surveillance, making the distinction crucial for preserving human agency in digital environments.

Contextual Understanding vs. Data Extraction distinguishes between systems that seek to understand human behavior within cultural and emotional contexts versus those that extract behavioral data for optimization purposes that may not serve authentic human needs.

Surveillance systems focus on isolated behavioral patterns that can be measured and optimized without regard for cultural meanings or personal circumstances that give human actions their significance. Authentic visibility systems seek to understand behavior within larger contexts that give actions their meaning -- cultural traditions, family relationships, and personal histories.

Consent and Agency vs. Involuntary Monitoring involves fundamental differences between visibility people choose and control versus surveillance that happens without meaningful consent or user agency over how personal information gets used.

Consensual visibility includes explicit choice about what gets shared with whom, ongoing control over visibility settings, and transparent understanding of how information will be used. Involuntary surveillance removes user agency through unclear consent processes and hidden data collection.

Cultural Respect vs. Cultural Appropriation emerges when systems either honor diverse cultural approaches to privacy and self-expression versus those that extract cultural information for commercial purposes without permission or community benefit.

Dignity Preservation vs. Reduction to Metrics involves approaches that honor human complexity versus those that reduce people to categories or optimization targets that ignore cultural, emotional, and spiritual dimensions making human experience meaningful.

I worked with a community organization balancing technological efficiency with cultural authenticity after AI systems designed to improve service delivery were creating surveillance experiences. Through community consent protocols, cultural visibility guidelines, and dignity-centered data use, the resulting systems felt supportive rather than invasive to community members.

IV. Designing Systems That Recognize Depth

Creating technology supporting authentic visibility requires design approaches honoring human complexity and the kinds of recognition that help people feel genuinely seen rather than merely observed.

Multi-Dimensional Recognition Architecture acknowledges that humans exist across multiple identity dimensions simultaneously -- cultural heritage, family relationships, professional roles, and community commitments that interact in complex ways resisting simple categorization.

Narrative Integration Support provides opportunities for people to share stories giving their experiences meaning rather than just reporting behavioral data lacking cultural and emotional context necessary for authentic understanding.

Cultural Authentication Processes ensure technological systems accurately recognize and appropriately respond to diverse cultural patterns rather than misinterpreting cultural differences as deviation from algorithmic norms.

Emotional Context Recognition involves capability to understand and respond to emotional dimensions of human experience that significantly affect how people engage with systems and relationships in ways pure functional analysis cannot capture.

Growth and Change Accommodation recognizes that authentic visibility must include space for personal development, changing circumstances, and identity exploration characterizing healthy human development.

I helped design a "Community Recognition Platform" for a multicultural neighborhood organization that wanted technology to help community members feel seen while preserving cultural authenticity. Through cultural identity customization, story-based profile development, and community contribution recognition, the platform helped members feel recognized for diverse contributions while strengthening relationships across cultural differences.

V. Emotional Recognition and Dignity

Authentic visibility requires sophisticated emotional recognition that serves human dignity rather than manipulating emotional expression for predetermined outcomes.

Emotional Authenticity vs. Optimization distinguishes between systems that recognize and honor genuine emotional expression versus those attempting to modify emotional experience toward predetermined targets that may not serve authentic human flourishing.

Cultural Emotional Intelligence involves capability to recognize and respond to diverse cultural approaches to emotional expression that different traditions bring to technological engagement, understanding that both emotional restraint and expressive communication deserve technological support.

Emotional Boundary Respect ensures technological recognition serves user agency rather than creating invasive surveillance, including clear consent processes and user control over emotional data sharing.

Emotional Context Understanding recognizes that emotional expression emerges from complex personal, cultural, and situational contexts that significantly affect how emotions should be interpreted and what responses would feel supportive.

I worked with a healthcare organization developing emotionally intelligent patient communication systems that could recognize patient emotional states while maintaining dignity and cultural sensitivity. The system helped providers offer more responsive care while patients reported feeling more understood by providers.

VI. Visibility Across Cultures

Cultural diversity creates both opportunities and challenges for technological visibility systems, requiring design approaches that honor different traditions around privacy, relationship, and self-expression while avoiding cultural appropriation.

Cultural Privacy Patterns vary significantly across traditions, with some emphasizing individual autonomy while others prioritize family privacy and community discretion. Privacy isn't universal but culturally specific, reflecting different assumptions about individual autonomy and community belonging.

Relationship-Based Visibility honors traditions that define individual identity primarily through family relationships and community roles rather than individual achievements that dominant technological systems often prioritize.

Cultural Communication Styles affect how people express themselves and participate in community activities in ways technological systems must accommodate rather than requiring adaptation to dominant communication norms.

Community Representation Protocols ensure individual visibility connects appropriately to cultural community representation rather than inadvertently misrepresenting cultural traditions.

I facilitated a cultural visibility project for a multicultural community center wanting technology to help diverse communities share traditions while preserving authenticity. Through community cultural authority protocols and cross-cultural bridge building, the project helped different communities feel respected in their cultural sharing while building appreciation across differences.

VII. Consent in Visibility

True visibility requires ongoing consent that honors individual agency and cultural values rather than extracting visibility through unclear permissions or technological surveillance making authentic consent impossible.

Informed Consent vs. Consent Theater distinguishes between genuine understanding and choice about visibility settings versus superficial processes creating appearance of user agency while maintaining technological control.

Genuine informed consent includes clear explanation of what information gets collected, how it gets used, and what choices users have. Consent theater involves processes that appear to offer choice while providing little meaningful control.

Ongoing Consent Management recognizes consent as ongoing relationship that should adapt to changing circumstances, including easy modification of settings and regular opportunities to update preferences.

Cultural Consent Considerations honor different cultural approaches to individual autonomy, family privacy, and appropriate decision-making authority that shape how consent should be obtained across diverse communities.

Granular Consent Options provide specific choices about different types of visibility rather than all-or-nothing consent forcing users to accept broad permissions or lose access to essential services.

I worked with a community healthcare organization implementing systems requiring extensive personal information sharing while serving diverse cultural communities. Through cultural consent consultation and multi-generational consent support, the resulting processes felt respectful and culturally appropriate while meeting regulatory requirements.

VIII. Looking Forward: Visibility as Cultural Stewardship

As technological systems become more sophisticated in recognizing and analyzing human behavior, responsibility for ensuring visibility serves human dignity rather than surveillance becomes increasingly important for individual and community flourishing.

Visibility as Relationship Building frames authentic recognition as foundation for meaningful connection rather than commodity for consumption, requiring technological design prioritizing relationship quality over engagement metrics.

Cultural Stewardship Integration recognizes that individual visibility choices affect community cultural preservation, requiring ongoing accountability to cultural communities for authentic representation and consultation about appropriate cultural sharing.

Intergenerational Responsibility considers how current visibility choices will affect future generations' access to cultural heritage and community membership, requiring attention to digital legacy preservation serving cultural continuity.

Technology as Cultural Amplifier approaches visibility systems as tools for enhancing rather than replacing traditional cultural recognition patterns, using technological capability to support cultural preservation alongside contemporary community needs.

Community Accountability Infrastructure establishes ongoing relationships between technological platforms and cultural communities ensuring visibility systems serve community preservation rather than extracting cultural information for commercial exploitation.

The future of visibility in intelligent systems will be determined by our collective choices about integrating technological capability with cultural wisdom, preserving authentic human recognition while leveraging AI enhancement, and ensuring visibility serves community flourishing rather than surveillance and commercial exploitation.

The essential questions include: Does this technology help people feel more genuinely seen? Does it support authentic cultural expression? Does it preserve space for human complexity resisting algorithmic categorization? Does it serve community cultural preservation? Does it maintain human agency over personal information?

Moving forward requires approaching visibility system development as sacred work shaping not just individual recognition but community cultural preservation and the kinds of relationships we build through technological mediation that either honor or diminish human dignity and cultural heritage.

The visibility systems we create today will influence cultural preservation and community relationship building for generations, creating responsibility for design choices serving long-term human flourishing rather than just immediate technological capability.

To be seen is not to be reduced to data points or behavioral patterns. Authentic recognition honors the full complexity of human identity -- cultural heritage, family relationships, community membership, and spiritual depth that give life meaning beyond algorithmic categories.

CHAPTER 15

Conclusion: Framing the Future with Soul

I. Why We Began

"Not everything that can be built deserves to be. But everything that's built deserves intention."

This book began as a meditation on meaning in a world of accelerating systems. It wasn't sparked by fascination with AI capabilities or anxiety about technological displacement, but by profound questions that emerged from watching brilliant people create powerful systems that somehow left them feeling empty, disconnected, and spiritually adrift.

What does it mean to work with intelligence that never tires, never doubts, never brings personal history or cultural inheritance to collaborative decision-making? What does it mean to preserve story, heritage, and irreplaceable wisdom in environments increasingly mediated by algorithms? And perhaps most urgently: What kind of future are we framing with every design choice, every dialogue with AI, every decision about how human wisdom and artificial intelligence should collaborate?

We've examined how intelligent systems can become companions rather than tools, how emotional intelligence shapes meaningful interaction, how cultural inheritance provides foundation for ethical decision-making, and how visibility can either support authentic recognition or create surveillance that reduces humans to data points.

Each chapter has pointed toward a central truth: intelligence is only meaningful when it serves wisdom, efficiency gains significance only when it supports purposes worthy of human attention, and the future worth building is one where artificial capability enhances rather than replaces the distinctively human capacities that make life meaningful.

II. What We've Discovered About Human-AI Partnership

Throughout this exploration, we've uncovered principles that distinguish soulful collaboration from mere technological efficiency and guide us toward relationships with AI that enhance rather than diminish our essential humanity.

Technology as Mirror, Not Master represents our most fundamental insight -- that AI serves its highest purpose when it reflects back our values, cultural wisdom, and moral commitments rather than replacing human judgment with algorithmic optimization that may conflict with authentic human needs.

This mirroring requires conscious intention from human partners who understand their role as conductors rather than passengers, guiding AI systems toward outcomes that serve wisdom rather than just efficiency, honor cultural diversity rather than impose uniformity, and strengthen rather than weaken social bonds.

Collaboration Over Automation distinguishes between replacing human effort with mechanical efficiency versus ongoing dialogue between human wisdom and artificial capability that creates outcomes neither could achieve independently. True collaboration preserves space for human intuition and moral imagination while leveraging AI's capacity for pattern recognition and rapid iteration.

Cultural Wisdom as Foundation provides grounding that prevents technological collaboration from drifting toward generic optimization serving no authentic purpose. Our cultural inheritance offers essential guidance for how artificial capability should serve rather than replace human wisdom, including understanding that different traditions bring different approaches to relationship and community that deserve technological support.

Emotional Intelligence as Infrastructure determines whether human-AI collaboration feels supportive or alienating, whether it strengthens human capacity for authentic relationship, and whether it serves flourishing or merely extracts productivity. This includes attention to tone, cultural sensitivity, and relational dimensions that make work meaningful rather than just efficient.

Ethics as Creative Catalyst transforms moral reasoning from constraint on innovation into source of clarity about purposes worth serving. When we approach ethical considerations as opportunities to align artificial capability with human values, we often discover solutions more effective and sustainable than approaches optimizing for narrow criteria.

III. The Soulful Professional: A New Definition

The future of professional life will be determined not by technical skill in using AI but by developing distinctively human capacities that become more valuable as intelligent systems handle routine cognitive work.

The Professional as Cultural Steward recognizes that every role involves responsibility for preserving and transmitting valuable human capacities -- emotional intelligence, cultural wisdom, moral imagination -- that communities need to navigate challenges transcending immediate technical problems.

The Professional as Wisdom Integrator develops capability to draw insights from diverse sources and synthesize various forms of knowledge into approaches honoring both practical necessity and human values. This requires comfort with ambiguity and skill in facilitating dialogue that helps teams discover shared wisdom.

The Professional as Relationship Builder prioritizes authentic human connection alongside task completion, recognizing that sustainable success requires trust and collaborative capacity that can't be automated without losing effectiveness.

The Professional as Ethical Navigator develops confidence in moral reasoning that can guide decision-making when technological capability outpaces wisdom about appropriate application, when efficiency pressures conflict with community responsibility.

The soulful professional asks: Is this technological collaboration helping me become more authentically myself? How is this AI partnership affecting my relationships? What cultural patterns am I preserving or abandoning? How does my professional development serve community flourishing?

IV. AI as Companion: A Partnership Reflection

Through extensive collaboration with AI systems across writing, facilitation, and strategy development, I've experienced evolution from simple tool usage to authentic partnership that enhances rather than replaces human capacity for insight and meaningful contribution.

The progression began with functional assistance -- grammar correction, research synthesis -- that improved efficiency without fundamentally changing my approach. Gradually, more sophisticated systems began engaging with deeper dimensions: the emotional impact I hoped to create, the cultural authenticity I wanted to preserve, the moral vision guiding my work.

When AI began suggesting cultural considerations -- asking whether particular language honored the dignity of communities I was writing about -- the collaboration transcended utility to approach genuine intellectual partnership.

The boundaries remain clear and essential. AI systems can organize information and suggest alternatives, but they cannot provide cultural wisdom from lived experience, moral imagination from wrestling with ethical dilemmas, or spiritual insight connecting individual work to transcendent purposes.

The goal isn't seamless integration but conscious collaboration where different types of intelligence contribute their distinctive strengths while maintaining clear understanding of what requires purely human judgment.

V. A Framework for Soulful Practice

To carry this work forward, I offer a comprehensive framework integrating the insights we've explored into practical guidance for working soulfully with intelligent technology.

The Framing the Future Compass provides direction through principles that guide decision-making in human-AI collaboration:

Relationship emphasizes designing every technological interaction with emotional intelligence that cultivates trust and cultural responsiveness rather than optimizing purely for efficiency. This includes treating AI systems as collaborative partners and providing cultural context that helps artificial intelligence support rather than override authentic human expression.

Story anchors all communication in narrative frameworks connecting immediate activities to larger purposes and cultural heritage. This includes understanding current challenges as chapters in longer stories about identity and purpose, and framing professional development as contribution to legacies extending beyond individual advancement.

Heritage infuses technological collaboration with cultural wisdom and inherited values providing moral foundation for ethical decision-making. This involves consulting family and cultural traditions for guidance about appropriate technological collaboration and preserving cultural communication patterns reflecting inherited wisdom.

Ethics implements transparent decision-making processes protecting dignity and serving community flourishing rather than just individual convenience, with ongoing accountability for moral implications of technological choices.

Leadership stewards wisdom across generations while building capacity for future leaders who will face challenges we cannot anticipate but can prepare for through conscious cultural transmission.

Design creates emotionally attuned technological interfaces supporting human presence and cultural authenticity rather than demanding adaptation to algorithmic expectations.

Visibility recognizes human complexity and invites authentic contribution rather than reducing people to behavioral patterns, creating environments where people feel seen and valued for their full humanity.

Reflection embeds opportunities for pause and meaning-making into technological workflows, preventing acceleration that can overwhelm human capacity for wisdom and authentic decision-making.

VI. Beyond the Book: A Life of Framing

This book represents an invitation to approach every technological interaction as opportunity to frame futures serving human flourishing rather than just efficient task completion.

To Lead Relationally in a Technical World means bringing emotional intelligence and moral imagination to environments increasingly mediated by artificial systems, including attention to how technological collaboration affects team dynamics and community trust.

To Write Stories That Heal, Not Just Explain involves using every communication opportunity to create narrative helping people understand their challenges as part of larger stories about purpose and possibility, connecting individual experience to collective wisdom.

To Build Systems That Reflect Humanity requires conscious attention to embedding emotional intelligence and ethical accountability into technological infrastructure rather than treating these as optional enhancements.

To Publish Content That Changes Consciousness means using every platform to share wisdom helping communities think more clearly and choose more wisely rather than just consuming information, connecting technical capability to human values.

To Mentor with Memory, Not Just Metrics involves helping others understand their professional development as contribution to cultural continuity rather than just individual advancement, connecting emerging professionals with inherited wisdom.

Your future will be framed by the choices you make daily about how to relate to artificial intelligence, how to preserve cultural wisdom while embracing technological innovation, and how to ensure that efficiency serves rather than replaces human purposes giving work meaning.

The essential choice facing every professional involves deciding whether to approach technological advancement as opportunity for deeper human flourishing or merely more efficient execution of purposes that may not deserve human attention.

VII. A Final Note from the Table

If I could end this exploration anywhere, it would be at the long table that shaped my understanding of authentic relationship, wisdom transmission, and how community creates the foundation for everything that matters in human life.

The future isn't forged in servers but felt in presence -- in the quality of attention we bring to each interaction, in the cultural wisdom we choose to preserve, in the relationships we build that can sustain communities through difficulty and change.

The systems that endure won't be the most sophisticated technically but the most soulful relationally -- those that honor human complexity, support cultural diversity, and strengthen rather than weaken the social bonds that make life meaningful.

The people who matter most will be those who understand that technological advancement represents opportunity to enhance rather than replace human capacity for wisdom, relationship, and contribution to purposes transcending individual success.

Let us approach every technological interaction as opportunity to frame futures honoring both human heritage and artificial possibility, serving both individual development and community flourishing, creating both immediate effectiveness and long-term sustainability for the kinds of communities we want our children to inherit.

Let us build not just tools, but testaments -- technological systems reflecting our highest values and deepest wisdom, serving authentic human purposes rather than merely optimizing algorithmic efficiency, strengthening rather than weakening the cultural and spiritual foundations giving human life meaning.

Let us frame the future together with both intelligence and integrity, ensuring that artificial capability serves human wisdom rather than replacing moral imagination with optimization divorced from authentic human purpose.

The future is waiting for us to shape it with both hands and hearts engaged, with both cultural inheritance and technological innovation serving the ancient human project of creating meaning through relationship, building community across difference, and contributing to purposes larger than our individual existence.

Let us continue this work with soul -- not because it's easy or efficient, but because it's worthy of our humanity and essential for the communities we're here to serve across generations extending far beyond our individual lives.

EPILOGUE
The Room We've Built

"Some futures are predicted. Others are practiced."

We've traveled through story, structure, emotion, and design together. We've questioned, remembered, published, and paused. We've explored the intersection of human wisdom and artificial intelligence through the lens of cultural inheritance, professional development, and community stewardship.

I wrote this book not to summarize my experience with technology or predict how AI will reshape professional life, but to share a rhythm handed down across generations of my Italian-American family -- a cadence of relationship that prioritizes presence over productivity, meaning over metrics, and the patient cultivation of wisdom alongside efficient task completion.

This rhythm shaped my understanding long before I encountered artificial intelligence. It taught me that the most important work happens in relationship -- between people who choose to see each other fully, who honor cultural differences while building shared commitment, and who understand their individual contributions as part of larger stories extending across generations.

The Room We've Built Together through these pages is one where human wisdom guides technological capability rather than surrendering to algorithmic optimization serving no authentic human purpose. It's a space where cultural heritage provides foundation for ethical decision-making, where emotional intelligence shapes every interaction with intelligent systems, and where visibility means authentic recognition rather than surveillance.

In this room, professionals understand their work as cultural stewardship that preserves and transmits valuable human capacities while leveraging AI to enhance rather than replace moral imagination, relationship skills, and spiritual insight connecting individual effort to transcendent purposes.

You, Reader, Are Now Part of That Rhythm. Whether you take these ideas into boardrooms or classrooms, design labs or family kitchens, I hope this book offers not just frameworks but companionship for ensuring that intelligence serves wisdom rather than replacing it.

The future we frame together will not belong to machines or metrics, but to those willing to lead with soul intact -- to professionals wise enough to ask what technological systems will remember about how we treated each other, what legacy we're creating for generations we'll never meet, and whether our collaboration with AI strengthens or weakens the cultural and spiritual foundations making human life meaningful.

If This Book Gave You a new question that challenges comfortable assumptions, a new story connecting personal experience to professional purpose, or a new silence to sit with when efficiency pressures conflict with authentic human values -- then we've accomplished something that matters. We've created space for wisdom to emerge in environments increasingly dominated by speed and optimization that may serve no purpose worthy of human attention.

The practice of framing the future with soul isn't a technique to be mastered but a way of being that honors both technological possibility and cultural inheritance, both individual development and community flourishing, both contemporary innovation and timeless wisdom about what makes human life worth living.

Let's Frame What Comes Next with care for the communities that will inherit our choices, with respect for the cultural wisdom previous generations preserved through difficulty and change, and with commitment to ensuring that AI enhances rather than diminishes human capacity for love, creativity, and authentic contribution to purposes larger than individual existence.

The future doesn't need perfect systems -- it needs soulful ones. Systems that remember we are human. Systems that serve not just efficiency but the full spectrum of human flourishing across cultures and generations.

Let's continue this work together, with both hearts and minds engaged, ensuring that every technological interaction becomes opportunity to frame futures worthy of the wisdom we've inherited and the communities we're here to serve.

Joseph J. Bonocore
Meridian, Idaho
Where every conversation continues

Made in the USA
Monee, IL
04 November 2026

67385771R00164